The Complete Guide to
ORGANIZING
YOUR RECORDS FOR
ESTATE
PLANNING

Step-by-Step Instructions
With Companion CD-ROM

By
John N. Peragine, Jr.

The Complete Guide to Organizing Your Records for Estate Planning: Step-by-Step Instructions With Companion CD-ROM

Copyright © 2009 Atlantic Publishing Group, Inc.
1405 SW 6th Avenue • Ocala, Florida 34471 • Phone 800-814-1132 • Fax 352-622-1875
Web site: www.atlantic-pub.com • E-mail: sales@atlantic-pub.com
SAN Number: 268-1250

ISBN-13: 978-1-60138-235-1   ISBN-10: 1-60138-235-9

Library of Congress Cataloging-in-Publication Data

Peragine, John N., 1970-
  The complete guide to organizing your records for estate planning : step-by-step instructions with companion CD-ROM / John N. Peragine, Jr.
     p. cm.
  Includes bibliographical references and index.
  ISBN-13: 978-1-60138-235-1 (alk. paper)
  ISBN-10: 1-60138-235-9 (alk. paper)
  1. Estate planning. 2. Finance, Personal. 3. Records--Management. I. Title.

  HG179.P365 2008
  332.024'016--dc22
                              2009008065

Printed in the United States

Printed on Recycled Paper

COVER DESIGN: Meg Buchner • megadesn@mchsi.com
PROJECT MANAGER: Melissa Peterson • mpeterson@atlantic-pub.com

We recently lost our beloved pet "Bear," who was not only our best and dearest friend but also the "Vice President of Sunshine" here at Atlantic Publishing. He did not receive a salary but worked tirelessly 24 hours a day to please his parents. Bear was a rescue dog that turned around and showered myself, my wife Sherri, his grandparents Jean, Bob and Nancy and every person and animal he met (maybe not rabbits) with friendship and love. He made a lot of people smile every day.

We wanted you to know that a portion of the profits of this book will be donated to The Humane Society of the United States.   *–Douglas & Sherri Brown*

The human-animal bond is as old as human history. We cherish our animal companions for their unconditional affection and acceptance. We feel a thrill when we glimpse wild creatures in their natural habitat or in our own backyard.

Unfortunately, the human-animal bond has at times been weakened. Humans have exploited some animal species to the point of extinction.

The Humane Society of the United States makes a difference in the lives of animals here at home and worldwide. The HSUS is dedicated to creating a world where our relationship with animals is guided by compassion. We seek a truly humane society in which animals are respected for their intrinsic value, and where the human-animal bond is strong.

Want to help animals? We have plenty of suggestions. Adopt a pet from a local shelter, join The Humane Society and be a part of our work to help companion animals and wildlife. You will be funding our educational, legislative, investigative and outreach projects in the U.S. and across the globe.

Or perhaps you'd like to make a memorial donation in honor of a pet, friend or relative? You can through our Kindred Spirits program. And if you'd like to contribute in a more structured way, our Planned Giving Office has suggestions about estate planning, annuities, and even gifts of stock that avoid capital gains taxes.

Maybe you have land that you would like to preserve as a lasting habitat for wildlife. Our Wildlife Land Trust can help you. Perhaps the land you want to share is a backyard—that's enough. Our Urban Wildlife Sanctuary Program will show you how to create a habitat for your wild neighbors.

So you see, it's easy to help animals. And The HSUS is here to help.

THE HUMANE SOCIETY OF THE UNITED STATES.

2100 L Street NW • Washington, DC 20037
202-452-1100 • www.hsus.org

Dedication

I dedicate this book to my loving wife, two beautiful daughters, Teeny and Izze. This book is part of my legacy to them.

Table Of Contents

Chapter 5: A List of Instructions about Your Estate — 55

Chapter 18: Last Words   175

Chapter 19: Will and Trust Information   181

Chapter 20: Insurance Policies   211

Chapter 28: Other Information 267

Chapter 29: Storage and Keeping Records Safe 273

Chapter 30: Conclusion 279

Appendix A: Case Studies 281

Appendix B: Answers to the Estate Planning Quiz 323

Appendix C: Veterinary Schools that Take Pets 327

Bibliography 331

Author Biography 332

Index 333

Foreword

As an estate planning attorney for 18 years, I witnessed numerous families struggle with the death of a loved one. The primary pain is loss, but that emotion can be eased by gratitude for the well-organized estate or enhanced by frustration for the financial chaos some people leave their loved ones. I had cases where the only way the executor or trustee learned of accounts and insurance polices was by waiting for statements in the mail. More than a few families have had to sort through hundreds of files of needless information to find a Will, an insurance policy, or a designation form. New clients often told me that they had an awful experience with the administration of a parent's estate and that they were hiring me to prevent doing the same thing to their children.

The Complete Guide to Organizing Your Records for Estate Planning: Step-by-Step Instructions by John Peragine describes every aspect of organizing financial, family, and health care matters. What can feel like a daunting task is broken down into easily achievable steps that will leave you, and your family, with a roadmap of your wishes. An estate planning attorney, accountant, and financial planner can help with the complex analysis of a plan, but they are not there in your home arranging your documents; that is your responsibility. This book is an excellent tool for giving your family and beneficiaries the gift of clarity of your wishes and ease of administration.

The sooner you start this process, the better. One advantage to starting relatively early in life is, generally, there is less financial information to organize and updating becomes a habit. Moreover, as John Peragine discusses in the first chapter, death will come to everyone and no one knows when. Particularly with regard to your health care decisions, clearly stating your wishes and appointing someone to direct them is imperative at every age because accidents happen. Sensitive health care matters become an issue when direction is absent, leaving the family, doctors, and sometimes a judge trying to determine your wishes.

For many people, seeing an attorney to document their estate plan will be necessary. As a former attorney, I found this book very helpful. First, estate planners will ask about your assets and their value, and after completing your portfolio, you will be able to accurately provide this information. Second, I found that most clients are not aware of estate planning options and terminology and can become overwhelmed by all of the information discussed in the first meeting. This book gives an introduction to estate planning topics, so hopefully, the first attorney meeting will not feel quite as daunting. Third, the book contains various suggestions for including personal messages and information. These mementos can be very meaningful to family and friends, but an attorney generally is not the appropriate person to consult in these matters.

Setting up a portfolio, as John Peragine describes, will be one of the last gifts you can leave your family, and in my experience, it will be one received with tremendous gratitude.

Kim L. Allen-Niesen, Esq.

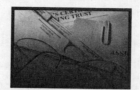

Introduction

There is only one thing that is inevitable in life, and that is death. It may be a depressing concept to face for some, but as the expression goes, the only things that you have to do in life are die and pay taxes. If you do not do your taxes, you may end up in prison, or you may be lucky enough to cheat on your taxes and get away with it. Unfortunately, there is no way to cheat death. It visits us all, whether we want it or not. For some, death is expected, and they have time to say their goodbyes and prepare. For others, death can come quickly and unexpected.

Everyone who owns any sort of property, assets in stocks, annuities, or pension funds needs to plan for an emergency that could have death or incapacitation as a result. Anyone with a child, extended family, or friends they wish to entrust their care and belongings to needs to prepare for an emergency, and the ultimate demise of life through death. On average, it can take a few weeks, or even months, to get things in order. It depends on the amount and types of assets you are dealing with.

Whoever said that you cannot take your belongings with you never spoke a truer word. The ancient Egyptians built large pyramids filled with a pharaoh's belongings, slaves, and wives to have in the afterlife. In order to build such a monument, they needed to plan ahead. In fact, they worked many years preparing for that final day. I am not suggesting you build a pyramid, but I am suggesting that you be as prepared as you can be.

If you are younger than retirement age, you may be ready to put this book down, thinking that you have years ahead of you. You are young, healthy, and have your whole life to live. As human beings, we do not have the ability to calculate our exact time of death. If we did, I believe that we would live our lives quite differently. This book is written for everyone over 18 years old. It is never too early to begin your estate planning. People in their 80's are more likely to be thinking seriously about preparing for their death, and to have begun the process of preparation, than someone much younger.

You could gamble that you have many years in front of you, and that you do not need to think of such morbid subjects as death, funerals, and estates. It is easier to gamble on our own lives than it is to gamble on the lives of those we love. It you do not prepare, or even think about your estate early, you are taking the chance that when you are gone, your loved ones will be left with a financial nightmare that is superimposed upon the grief of losing you.

Preparation of your estate should not be stressful or depressing. Instead, you should think of it as a labor of love. You are taking care of your family and friends for a time that you will not be able to physically. Having a well organized estate is a love letter to them stating that you cared enough about them to make sure every detail was covered so that the transition would be as smooth and simple as possible.

Most people do not want to think about the problems their spouse and children could endure while waiting on your assets that could be frozen by the bank or court system. They could wait months or years for the money to be released, while still being responsible for paying the mortgage or other expenses. The more work you do today, the less hassle and heartache it will cause your loved ones later. This book will help you every step of the way and can save you thousands of dollars in accounting and attorney fees. Give your family a gift that will last for years, and even generations, by beginning to organize and prepare your estate.

There are many things you can do on your own, such as organizing records, gathering information, and making major decisions about your estate. There may be situations in which you will need to talk to accounting professionals, lending experts, or even an attorney. Having this book and using the information will result in you paying much less for these types of professionals. In addition, if you already have the necessary documents ready to go, you will not have to pay someone else to research and gather them for you. Saving money now will mean you will have more to invest later, which can mean leaving your family a little extra, or having enough to go on a fantastic vacation this summer.

Another reason for this book is to help you in case you are ever incapacitated. If you are not able to handle your affairs, no matter the reason, having everything in order can be a blessing for your family. You should read through this book carefully, and try not to skip any sections. It is the small details that can become a burden later on.

> The biggest villain in estate planning is not the IRS;
> It's procrastination!
>
> Mike Kilbourn, Kilbourn Associates

Suppose you have done all the work and placed all your necessary documents in a safety deposit box. You may believe you have thought about all the necessary arrangements, but suppose you forgot to tell your family where the key for the box is? If they have the key, do they know which bank the box is located in? If they show up with key in hand, will they be able to access your box? Have you given your family members the necessary permissions to access these important documents? This book will help you address all these issues.

You may also have purchased this book because you have been entrusted with or are concerned with the affairs of your parents or aging family member. This book can help you make all the necessary arrangements to help make their transition easier and ensure that all their personal affairs are in order.

Whatever your reason for buying this book, you will be glad you did. This book was created to be accessible to the general public in hopes that everyone will find information that will help them deal with situations that, while not always pleasant to think about, are necessary.

> Make a checklist of items, and keep these in a life-planning binder. This should include your doctors' names, where they practice, and related information. The list is endless and needs to include everything someone would need to know if you weren't able to tell them. Have you purchased a cemetery plot? Have you made funeral arrangements? Who does your car, bank account, child, or pet go to?
>
> Barry Friefield, Tax Partner, CPA, Abalos & Associates, P.C.

In this book, and on the CD-ROM, you will find various forms and documents that will help you create a portfolio of materials to help you get your affairs taken care of and organized. I recommend making copies of the forms first and using pencil to work on them. Once you are satisfied with the information, you can either copy the pages or write on them with ink, or you can print them out from the CD-ROM. If you do decide to print them out, make sure you initial and date each page. You do not want anyone questioning the authenticity of the documents during the time when they will be the most important.

You may wish to get some of the forms you create for your portfolio notarized. In some situations, you will need help filling out documents, or a lawyer may need to assist you in drawing up papers. Doing most of the work yourself does not mean that the documents are any less valid than if you had an attorney do them. You just want to make sure that you are filling out the correct documents in a complete fashion. If you are filling in the documents yourself, you must be sure that your writing is clear and legible.

Once you have filled out all the necessary documents, it is still necessary to update some of the forms on a regular basis, as your assets may have grown or changed. Only your most current documents will be considered in a will. If you need to change items, such as beneficiaries, do so immediately. Just because you mentioned that you intended to change something on a form to someone does not mean that their word will be taken over a written, signed document. When you update your forms, make sure you remove the older forms from your portfolio and destroy them. This will reduce confusion for your loved ones later.

CHAPTER 1

What Do You Need Before You Begin?

The Portfolio

In this section, you will learn how to create a portfolio that will contain all the information and documents that your loved ones will need. Because it is a good idea to keep all your documents in one place, I suggest you purchase two plastic, two-inch, three-ring binders. Having two binders with the same information can ensure that if something happens to the first one, your loved ones will not be at a total loss, as there is a copy someplace else.

If you decide to create a copy of your portfolio, it is essential that both binders contain the exact same information. If you update your materials, make sure you update both portfolios. If the portfolios contain outdated or conflicting information, it can cause confusion later on.

In addition to the binders, you may want to purchase a three-hole punch so that you can place your documents securely in your portfolio. You should have some tab-divider pages on hand to separate the sections of your portfolio. You can add pocket-divider pages and plastic sleeves to have a place to store documents that you do not want to punch holes in. If you want to add other items such as keys or credit cards to your portfolio, add a plastic binder pouch with a zipper.

You will be glad that you created a portfolio when you have completed it. You will feel content that you have an organized folder of your documents and instructions that will be the guide to help your loved ones who will be struggling to deal with your death. Even though you will not be there to hear it, your family will be thankful for your thoughtful effort.

If you are creating this portfolio for a loved one, there is no better gift than the peace of mind that you will have given them. Be careful; if you have done a good job, you may find other friends and family asking you to create one for them. Everyone can benefit from getting their affairs in order, and not waiting until it is too late to worry about it.

> Everyone should have an estate-planning booklet that spells out what they would like to have happen at their death. It is so difficult for family members to have to make important decisions during an emotional time, and basic planning could make it so much easier for everyone. Especially if there are things that a person wants done, such as having a special friend speak at their funeral or a certain minister or musician participate, this needs to be in writing. Even if a family tries to fulfill one's wishes, they may not remember everything. Also, there may be cherished items that you would want to go to certain people, if you don't write that down, it may not happen. Also, don't forget your pets. Who would you like to take care of them and how much money will you allot for the care?
>
> Jane S Eddy, ChFC, CLU

The Portfolio

The portfolio sections that I recommend in this book are the areas that you or your loved ones will have to deal with when managing an estate. There will be sections that will apply to your situation and others that do not. You must decide which sections apply to your particular life situation and financial needs. Each section should be separated by a tab divider, and there should be a label filled out for each section. This will make it easier for someone using your portfolio to locate the information they are looking for. You may want to consider putting a table of contents or an index into your portfolio. You may also consider listing the contents of each section on the divider page, so the reader knows what is contained in a particular section. These ideas may seem a little labor intensive, but you will find, as you are creating or updating a portfolio, that having the sections labeled or having an index will help you figure out where to place a particular document. When someone is using the portfolio, they may take documents out. It is much easier if they know which section to place the items back into, and in what order.

Below is a list of different sections that I recommend that you have in your portfolio. You do not have to place them in the same order as I list them. Choose whichever way makes it easiest for you to organize your documents. Keep your organizing simple and logical.

1. **Your biography:** This section will contain information about your life. This includes your birth date, your birth city, places you have lived, marriages, children, and any other pertinent information. This is a good place to put a quick reference page that will contain all your vital information. You may even want to include a family tree, which will be discussed later on in the book. This is a wonderful legacy to leave your family. This section can include pictures of you at various points of your life, as well as pictures of relatives and people contained in your family tree.

2. **A letter to those you love:** In a later chapter, I will describe creating this letter. This is a goodbye letter, but also one of hope and love. You should make this letter easily seen and accessible so that it is one of the first things your loved ones will find in your portfolio.

3. **A list of instructions about your estate:** This list should be put toward the front of your book, as it will contain your wishes about funeral arrangements and other instructions about your wishes, should you no longer be able to make decisions for yourself.

4. **Your children:** This section will contain documents and instructions about your children. This section is especially important should you want to give instructions about who should care for them. You may want to include special letters for each of your children here.

5. **Care of others:** There may be other people who depend on you, such as friends, family, or even neighbors. In this section, you will insert instructions about how their care should be handled in your absence.

6. **Pets:** This section will contain all the necessary information about your pets' care and well-being.

7. **Employment:** This section will have documents related to your employment status. You may decide to place insurance information here, in another section, or both. You should at least have contact information for your boss and about whom to contact about benefits. You should include all the necessary paperwork about benefits and your income in this section.

8. **Business ownership:** This is a list of and documents related to businesses you own or have interests in. Make sure you include where these interests are located.

9. **Clubs and other organizations:** This section would include memberships, locations of those memberships, and any accrued benefits of those memberships.

10. **List of service providers:** This is a list of service providers, such as doctors, dentists, therapists, counselors, or specialists. You should list who they are, what they provide, and where they are located.

11. **Life support information:** In a later section, you will learn about medical directives in more detail. For now, just be aware that this section should be in your portfolio, and the information contained in this section should be easily accessible in case of an emergency.

12. **Power of Attorney:** This section should contain information about who has power of attorney, or who should be given power of attorney, over your finances should you become incapacitated.

13. **Organ donor:** If you plan to donate your organs, you should have instructions about where and to whom you are donating.

14. **Burial arrangements:** You should have a section, or at least clear instructions, about your funeral arrangements. Do you intend to be buried or cremated? Do you already have a plot? You should have all this information contained in one section in your portfolio.

15. **Funeral decisions:** Where do you wish to have your funeral? Do you have any special instructions? Whom do you wish to officiate? Do you want anything read at the funeral?

16. **Last words:** This section should contain an obituary, if you wish, and instructions on how you want it distributed and where.

17. **Will and trust information:** This should contain your actual will and testament. In addition, it should contain any trusts you wish to have set up and what they are to contain. This section would also contain any nuptial agreements or property settlement instructions.

18. **Insurance policies:** This section would contain all your insurance policies, beneficiaries, and agent contact information.

19. **Automobile and other vehicle information:** This section should contain information about all your vehicles, boats, RVs, or even planes you may own. It should contain the location, insurance policy information, registration information, and information regarding any banks that hold loans on the vehicles.

20. **Debts:** This section will contain information about loans and credit cards. It may not have current balances, but it should have payment information and account numbers.

21. **Social Security Benefits:** This section will contain information about Social Security benefits, Medicaid, Medicare, or any other government assistance you may be receiving. It should have account numbers and any information about direct deposit.

22. **Bank accounts:** This section should have the account numbers and locations of all your bank and brokerage accounts. It should have phone numbers, branch addresses, and approximate amounts. If you have CDs, IRAs, or any other bank investments, you should have them listed here.

23. **Employment pensions and retirement benefits:** This section will include the amounts of these benefits and pensions, the account numbers, and where they are coming from.

24. **Real estate ownership:** You should list all the real estate that you may own and where it is located. If there are loans on these properties, this information should be included.

25. **Tax information:** This kind of information will help loved ones pay your taxes.

26. **Other information:** You can have a section that is designated for any other information that you deem important. You can include family recipes, your fondest memories, or anything you wish to leave behind to your friends and family.

> It is rarely too soon to get your estate in order, especially if someone is eager to get things in order. Once a person is working and on their own, it is a good idea to have a will and medical directives drawn up.
>
> Jane S Eddy, ChFC, CLU

Quick Portfolio

Each of the sections above will be dealt with in the rest of this book. There are some areas that should be dealt with first if you need to create a portfolio quickly:

- Life support information

- Your children

- Organ donor status

- Funeral decisions

- Burial arrangements

- Will and trust information

- Insurance policies

- Bank accounts

Timelines of Your Portfolio

Some sections may take longer than others to complete because there may be more research involved, and you may have to wait to have something you requested sent to you. If you and your spouse decide that you want portfolios, you should create separate ones. There may be some crossover of documents, and that is all right, but certain areas will be handled differently for each of you.

Here are the simpler tasks that can be tackled first and do not require as much research or wait time:

- Your children

- Care of others

- Pets

- Club and other organizations

After you have dealt with those four tasks, you can move on to the following:

- Biography

- Employment

- Business ownership

- Last words

- Insurance policies

- Bank accounts

- Employment pensions and retirement benefits

- Social Security benefits

- Debts

- Tax information

- Real estate ownership

- Automobile and other vehicle information

- Other information

Once you have gathered all of these materials, and have placed them in the appropriate sections of your portfolio, you are left with the final tasks:

- A letter to those you love

- A list of instructions about your estate

When your portfolio is completed, it will then be time to store it and talk to your loved ones. Tell them what is contained in your portfolio, and let them know where you have stored it. If there is a copy of the portfolio, place it in another secure place, and let your loved ones know about that as well. Make sure that you update information in your portfolio on a regular basis and that you are making the corrections exactly the same in both copies.

CHAPTER 2

How Much Do You Know About Estate Planning

If you think you know everything about estate planning, then I invite you to take the quiz below. If you are like most people, you may not know as much as you think, and what you do not know can cost you and your family thousands of dollars. Worst than that, it can add to your family's stress during a time when they may be emotionally overwrought.

Take the quiz, and then see how you did. The good news is that you will learn about all the different areas in this quiz throughout this book, so do not feel bad about not doing well. Try taking the quiz again after you have read and worked through the book, and see how your knowledge and understanding have grown.

Estate Planning Quiz

You will have a number of True/False (T/F) questions, multiple-choice questions, and fill-in-the-blank questions. You can find the answers in Appendix B of this book.

1. Estate planning requires an attorney.
   ❏ *True*   ❏ *False*

2. You are required to be embalmed when you are being buried.
    ❑ *True*   ❑ *False*

3. You are required to buy a casket at the funeral home you have chosen to use.
    ❑ *True*   ❑ *False*

4. If you are cremated, you are not allowed to have your ashes scattered in a public place.
    ❑ *True*   ❑ *False*

5. If you have property transferred to a trust, it must still go through probate.
    ❑ *True*   ❑ *False*

6. There is no such thing as an oral will.
    ❑ *True*   ❑ *False*

7. You have to pay taxes on any monetary gifts you give, no matter the amount.
    ❑ *True*   ❑ *False*

8. A doctor has to follow your medical directives.
    ❑ *True*   ❑ *False*

9. A will must be typed and signed in order to be valid.
    ❑ *True*   ❑ *False*

10. You must state whom you want as a guardian in your will.
    ❑ *True*   ❑ *False*

11. Once you have your will and durable power of attorney done, regardless of where you may move, it is valid in all 50 states and the District of Columbia.
    ❏ *True*   ❏ *False*

12. A _____ proceeding is required with a will.
    A. trust
    B. will
    C. probate
    D. none of the above

13. A(n) _____ is a trust that allows you to bypass probate hearings concerning a particular property.
    A. Irrevocable Land Trust
    B. Revocable Living Trust
    C. Time Stamped Trust
    D. none of the above

14. The creation of a _____ is possible with the carbon from cremation ashes.
    A. model
    B. diamond
    C. clone
    D. none of the above

15. You can _____ a casket for a viewing.
    A. steal
    B. hang
    C. rent
    D. none of the above

16. You can lose around _____ percent of your property in probate hearings.
    A. 20
    B. 50
    C. 75
    D. none of the above

17. A _____ is a type of fraternal membership.
    A. Water Buffalo Order
    B. Jaycee
    C. Freemason
    D. none of the above

18. A(n) _____ is another name for a handwritten will.
    A. laser
    B. holographic
    C. ethical
    D. none of the above

19. You can put a body _____ instead of embalming.
    A. on ice
    B. in a special chemical soup
    C. there is no substitute
    D. none of the above

20. A _____ is a large party to celebrate a person's life.
    A. wake
    B. visitation
    C. viewing
    D. none of the above

21. A _____ allows you to name someone while you are alive to take care of your financial matters, should you become incapacitated.
    A. medical power of attorney
    B. durable power of attorney for finances
    C. revocable living trust
    D. none of the above

22. A(n) _____ is a set of instructions of what to do if you should become incapacitated and unable to make medical decisions.

23. A(n) _____ is in charge of handling your affairs after you die.

24. A(n) _____ agreement occurs before a couple is married and can impact a person's estate.

25. A(n) _____ trust allows a couple to pass on their estate only after both spouses have died. It is a trust that helps prevent federal estate taxes from being levied.

26. It is a good idea to assign someone to care for your pet. There are some _____ schools that will take them and take care of them.

27. What assets escape probate without any real action on your part?

28. _____ donation can be done for medical research at a university.

29. A(n) _____ is a place where urns can be stored.

30. A(n)_____ account is a bank account that can allow funds to be released upon your death.

31. A(n)_____ is someone who is chosen to carry a casket.

32. Being _____ is a state in which you cannot make decisions for yourself.

33. Does everyone pay estate taxes?

34. Can I simply gift away all my possessions before I die?

35. Is it possible to make a change to an Irrevocable Trust that has already been established?

36. Can a parent sign legal documents, handle business affairs, or make medical decisions for their adult children?

37. For Medicaid purposes, is a transfer of not more than $12,000 annually allowed?

38. Does a will completely avoid probate?

39. If both parents die, and there are minor children, who has priority for the judge to pick as guardian?

CHAPTER 3

A Letter to Those You Love

The letter you write in this section should be the first thing your loved ones will read should you become incapacitated in some way or die. While it is the first thing in the portfolio, it will actually be the last thing you do in preparing your portfolio. It is one of the most important items, so take your time creating your letter.

Your letter will serve a few different purposes. One purpose is that it is the instruction manual for using your portfolio. It will also contain special messages to your loved ones and words of comfort. It may contain your thoughts on death and dying and your last thoughts and words for the world to hear.

To help you create your own letter, below you will find a simple template of the sections of your letter. This can be a difficult and emotional task for some people. Have the thoughts you want to be included, and you can direct these words to one person, or a select group of people. It can be as simple or elaborate as you choose. Just make sure it is purposeful and meaningful and expresses the things you want to say to your loved ones at the time when they need to hear your words the most.

Dear_____

Why: This is an explanation of why they are reading this letter, such as, you have died or have become incapacitated.

My Instructions: In this section, you will describe how to use the portfolio and what its purpose is. The section should contain step-by-step instructions that are easy to read, understand, and execute. Be detailed and structured in your instructions.

Death: In this section, you will describe your feelings and ideas about life, death, and the afterlife. You should talk about your hopes and fears concerning these subjects. Allow those who read this to find comfort that you will be alright and in a better state. You can talk about looking forward to meeting loved ones that have passed before you or about your religious visions of the afterlife.

Messages: In this section, you will write to specific people who are important to you. These are messages and words of love and comfort that you are leaving behind. Make sure they are personal and from your heart.

Last Thoughts: In this section, you will have some last words and thoughts as you pass from this world. You can use a quote or create words of your own. These are your final thoughts for the world to hear.

Signature

_____

If you do not feel comfortable writing a letter, you can create an audio or visual letter to your loved ones. There are books at your local library or bookstore that talk about creating last letters and love letters to your family and friends.

CHAPTER 4

Your Biography

> Everyone who is 18 or over should have incapacity documents, so if they are in an accident or have some tragedy strike, someone will be empowered to make decisions for them. A will or trust should be done if they have children, have more than minimal assets, or wish to leave their assets to people other than those listed in their state's intestacy statutes.
>
> Glenn A. Jarrett, Esq., CFP®, Jarrett Law Office, PLC

After your letter, your portfolio will be broken into various sections, each of them separated for easy access. Each of the following chapters will contain information about the various sections in your portfolio. You will find a description of the section, what should be contained in that section, suggestions for obtaining the information, and samples of forms and documents that belong in a particular section. Each of the forms can also be found on the CD-ROM that accompanies this book.

In the biography section of your portfolio, you will include all the important information about your life. It will have a fact sheet that contains all your vital information. This sheet will be used considerably by your loved ones, so make sure it is always accurate and up to date. On the next page is a sample fact sheet.

Fact Sheet

Name	Address	Lived at Address Since?
Date Of Birth	Telephone Number	Social Security Number
Mother's Maiden Name		Drivers License Number
Employer	Employer Address	Employer Phone Number

Children

Name		
Address		
Phone Number		

Spouse

Name	Address	Phone Number
Date of Birth	Date of Marriage	Date of Death

Physician

Type of Doctor			
Name			
Phone Number			
Prescribed Medications			

Once you have completed the fact sheet, you may move on to other important biographical information. The information in this section may be needed for contact information concerning the funeral and the will. This section contains important names and numbers of relatives and loved ones who should be contacted, or not contacted, in the event of your death.

My Biographical Information

Full Name (including middle and maiden names)
Date of Birth
Place of Birth
Social Security Number
Driver's License Number
Other Names Known By:

My Military Record

Military Service (branch, location, and rank)	Military Service (branch, location, and rank)	Military Service (branch, location, and rank)	Military Service (branch, location, and rank)
Dates Served	Dates Served	Dates Served	Dates Served
Military Honors	Military Honors	Military Honors	Military Honors

My Biological Parents

My Biological Mother

Name (including maiden name)	Address
Birth Date	Phone Number
Place of Birth	Date of Death
Military Service (branch, location, and rank)	Military Honors

My Biological Father

Name (including maiden name)	Address
Birth Date	Phone Number
Place of Birth	Date of Death
Military Service (branch, location, and rank)	Military Honors

My Stepparents (If Applicable)

My Stepmother

Name (including maiden name)	Address
Birth Date	Phone Number
Place of Birth	Date of Death
Military Service (branch, location, and rank)	Military Honors

My Stepfather

Name (including maiden name)	Address
Birth Date	Phone Number
Place of Birth	Date of Death
Military Service (branch, location, and rank)	Military Honors

My Prior Marriages (If Applicable)

1st Marriage

Name (including maiden name)	Address
Birth Date	Phone Number
Place of Birth	Date of Death
Date of Marriage	Date of Divorce or Separation

2nd Marriage

Name (including maiden name)	Address
Birth Date	Phone Number
Place of Birth	Date of Death
Date of Marriage	Date of Divorce or Separation

3rd Marriage

Name (including maiden name)	Address
Birth Date	Phone Number
Place of Birth	Date of Death
Date of Marriage	Date of Divorce or Separation

My Current Spouse or Long-Term Partner

Name (including maiden name)	Address
Birth Date	Phone Number
Place of Birth	Date of Death
Date of Marriage	Date of Divorce or Separation

My Employment

Name of Employer	Address	Phone Number
Date Employed	Date Retired	Contact Person
If Applicable		
Name of Employer	Address	Phone Number
Date Employed	Date Retired	Contact Person

My Children

Child 1

Name of Employer	Address
Birth Date	Phone Number
Place of Birth	Date of Death
Military Service (branch, location, and rank)	Military Honors

Child 2

Name of Employer	Address
Birth Date	Phone Number
Place of Birth	Date of Death
Military Service (branch, location, and rank)	Military Honors

Child 3

Name of Employer	Address
Birth Date	Phone Number
Place of Birth	Date of Death
Military Service (branch, location, and rank)	Military Honors

My Grandchildren

Name of Employer	Address
Birth Date	Phone Number
Place of Birth	Date of Death
Military Service (branch, location, and rank)	Military Honors

My Siblings

Name of Employer	Address
Birth Date	Phone Number
Place of Birth	Date of Death
Military Service (branch, location, and rank)	Military Honors

My Nieces or Nephews

Name of Employer	Address
Birth Date	Phone Number
Place of Birth	Date of Death
Military Service (branch, location, and rank)	Military Honors

Name of Employer	Address
Birth Date	Phone Number
Place of Birth	Date of Death
Military Service (branch, location, and rank)	Military Honors

Other Important People to Notify

Name	Address
Relation	Phone Number
Name	Address
Relation	Phone Number
Name	Address
Relation	Phone Number

People Who Should Not Be Contacted

Name	Reason Not to Notify

Once you have filled this information out, you will need to gather certain documents (listed below) that should be included in this section of your portfolio. The documents can have holes punched and be locked into the three-ring binder, or they can be slipped into a divider pocket. If they are not locked in, have them are stapled together. Make copies of these papers in case they get lost.

Birth Certificate

In your portfolio, you need to have a certified birth certificate, which you will need to request from the state in which you were born. When requesting the certificate, you will need your full birth name, date of birth, and county and city in which you were born. It will also be helpful to have your mother and father's full names, as they would appear on the birth certificate. You can then find on the Internet where you need to send your request, as each state, and even county, can be different. You may have to pay a fee for the certified copy.

Throughout this book, I will often emphasize that certain documents and information need to be kept in a secure place. In this age of the Internet and identity theft, certain records, such as your birth certificate, can be used for fraudulent purposes. Make sure you lock your birth certificate and any copies in a safe location, like a safe or safety deposit box.

Social Security Card

You need to have at least a copy of your social security card in your portfolio. You can place it in a zippered bag in your portfolio, if you wish. Like your birth certificate, this is an item that must be protected at all costs. You should never carry your social security card in your wallet.

If you do not have a copy of your social security card, you can apply for one at **http://www.ssa.gov/**. Do not use other sites that claim to help you get a social security card, and never give someone your social security number online or over the phone. If a crook has your social security card and birth certificate, he or she can ruin you financially.

You can also call 800-772-1213 to request an application, or you can go to your local social security office. You will need certain verifications to complete the application, so you may want to get your birth certificate first. You have to send in your original verification documents if you make the application by mail, but they will promptly send them back.

If you are not a natural born citizen or citizen of the United States, you may want to obtain your naturalization or citizenship certificates. These can be obtained by completing an N-565, which is the Application for Replacement Naturalization/Citizen Document. You can obtain this form from **www.uscis.gov/files/form/N-565.pdf**. There are attached instructions about how to fill it out and where to send it. If you are searching for paperwork for a loved one, you must use a Form G-639, which can be obtained at **www.uscis.gov/files/form/g-639.pdf**. As with the prior form, there are instructions attached.

Adoption Record

Many people are shocked at a funeral because they discover that the deceased was adopted. There may be questions, although some of them may never be answered. There are open adoptions, in which information about a biological family can be obtained, and there are closed adoptions, in which no information can be obtained. In order to help your family through this process, you could consider checking with the Child Welfare Information Gateway at **www.childwelfare.gov**, or you can call them, at 888-251-0075. They may be able to help you locate the records you are looking for. One of the main reasons that your family may want this information has to do with genetics. If there are any disorders or conditions that are prevalent in your biological family, this information may be important to pass on to your children and grandchildren.

Church Records

In some religious denominations, the records of being baptized can be very important. This can be important in the Catholic Church when it comes to last rites and whether you can be buried on hallowed ground. If you have trouble finding the particular church in which you were baptized, you can contact the regional office, and they may have the records or at least be able to put you in touch with the people who do.

Marriage License and Divorce Decrees

These records can be important, especially when there are claims about assets when the will is read. Make sure that you have all marriage, divorce, and annulment records contained in this section. You can usually obtain a marriage certificate if you know the county you were married in. You can contact vital records from that county, or you can sometimes find an application for a copy of the marriage certificate online. Make sure you know your spouse's full name, date of birth, and date of the marriage. If you know the city and county of your spouse's birth, that can be useful as well.

In cases of divorce or annulment, you must know which county these were granted in. You will need the date the divorce or annulment was granted and the full names of the people involved. If you have the date of the marriage, this will help them locate it easier. If you are still having difficulties finding the divorce, marriage, or annulment certificates, you can try the National Center for Health Statistics at **www.cdc.gov/nchs**.

If you are looking for an annulment that occurred in a Catholic church, you will need to contact the diocese in which the annulment occurred. There may be a small fee for an annulment certificate.

Military Records

These are important records to gather. Not only are they useful for benefits for your family, but they are also important so future generations can know about your service to the military. It is important that you seek out the record, because only you can have full access to your record while you are alive. Your next of kin may obtain records after your death, but these records may not be complete.

One option for obtaining military records can be found at the US National Archives and Records Administration (NARA). This organization maintains records for veterans who have served after the dates that are listed below.

	Enlisted:	Officers:
Navy	1884	1901
Army	October 31, 1912	June 29, 1917
Marine Corps	1905	1904
Coast Guard	1905	1897

You can begin accessing records if you are next of kin at **www.archives.gov**. You can download a request form, called a Standard Form 180, from the site or contact NARA at the address listed below:

National Personnel Records Center
Military Personnel Records
9700 Page Blvd
St. Louis, Missouri 63132-5100
Telephone Number: 866-325-7208.

Another option for obtaining records is the National Archives Building in Washington, DC. They have older records than NARA. You can order a record by submitting an NATF Form 86 from **www.archives.gov**. If you need to send the request by mail, you can do so at:

> National Archives and Records Administration
> Attention: NWCTB
> 700 Pennsylvania Ave. NW
> Washington, DC 20408-0001

Death Certificates

You may wish to add death certificates of immediate family members to this section. Like other documents listed in this section, you must know which county the death certificate will be located in. You must also know the person's full name and date of death. Having other items, such as the person's social security number, can also be helpful. You can then contact the vital records office in that county to obtain a record. It can sometimes be weeks before a death certificate is released, as it must be signed by the coroner.

Pictures and Memorabilia

You do not want to turn your portfolio into a scrapbook, but you may want to place some important pictures in this section. In the age of digital copies and pictures, you may even decide to place a CD into a pocket here. That way, you can store hundreds of pictures in a small space. Label your CD, and possibly create an index on it.

It might be a good idea to include pictures of you at different stages and important events in your life. You can include pictures of ancestors, siblings, and offspring. Make sure you label each picture, and include place and date if you can to make the memory more helpful and exciting for your loved ones. Your thoughtful gesture will be appreciated.

If there are too many pictures or memorabilia to place in your portfolio, make sure you leave a note in the section on where these materials are located. If you have the time and can create some scrapbooks, these are treasures people will love and appreciate for generations.

Family Tree

A family tree can be as elaborate or as simple as you wish. There are many family-tree-making programs on the market. With these programs, you can just place names and dates on a family tree, or have other detailed information, like military records and other interesting facts about your ancestors. I do recommend at least a one-page family tree that has you in the middle. Above you should be your parents and grandparents, as well as your spouse's parents and grandparents. Below you should be your children and grandchildren. A good place to get ideas, and even information about your family, is **www.ancestory.com**. There is a subscription fee for using this service.

In addition to your family tree, you can write a brief description of your life. It can be a couple of pages, or you could even turn it into a book. If you are not good at writing, you can record yourself on audio or video and have a relative interview you. For around $500, you could hire a personal historian to create a memoir for you. Contact the Association of Personal Historians, at **www.personalhistorians.com**, to find more information.

The biographical section of your portfolio is the section that will need the most updates. You may move, get married, have a child, lose a partner, or have other changes in your life, and you would need to update this section. You should commit that on each birthday, you will bring out your portfolio and update and review the information contained therein.

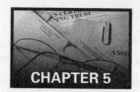

CHAPTER 5

A List of Instructions about Your Estate

Estate Planning should be accomplished while you are young and healthy. Do not wait until it's too late. Estate planning is also an ongoing process; it is not a "one and done" type affair. Your estate plan should be reviewed every year. Funding should be reviewed, the status of named individuals in the estate plan should be reviewed, family situation should be reviewed, and powers of attorney should be re-executed every few years.

Christopher J. Berry, Esq, Witzke Berry PLLC

In your letter to your family, you will have instructions about how to use the portfolio. You should refer them to this section of your binder, as it will contain detailed instructions about arrangements and how you want your affairs handled. This is different from your will in a couple of ways. First, this will not be a legal document, and second, it will be instructions about what you need done rather than who gets what.

Below is a sample document that you would want to include in this section. Again, you must assume that those reading your instructions have no idea what is going on or where things are located. In addition, the people reading this section may be in shock and may not comprehend things as easily.

When writing this document, you should make sure that your instructions are sequential. You can start with the first few days, then weeks, and then months. Each section will have instructions on what needs to be done, how to do it, who is involved, and where to find the materials needed to complete the tasks. The materials should mostly be contained in the portfolio, but if not, there should be instructions on where they can be found and how to access them.

Portfolio Instructions

To Whom it May Concern,

This is the master list of instructions on how to handle my estate should I be incapacitated and unable to handle my affairs, or in the event of my death. I have broken down the instructions into three sequential sections: the first week, the second week, and the first month. If at all possible, do not skip anything because I have given considerable thought to each item, and each item is important. I have done as much preparation as possible to make these tasks as easy as possible. I know you will be able to handle these tasks, and that is why I have chosen you to handle my affairs.

In Case I Am Incapacitated

If I am incapacitated, please turn to the section in this portfolio (**Chapter 14**) that deals with Health Care Directives and Durable Power of Attorney for my finances. I have given detailed instructions and have chosen whom I want to handle my affairs should I be incapacitated and no longer able to make decisions.

First Two Days

These are tasks that need to be taken care of right away. They should be completed within 48 hours of my death, if at all possible. I have given you a task and where to find the information and the documents that you will need to complete that task.

> Care my Children (**Chapter 6**)
> Care for other People (**Chapter 7**)
> Care for my Pets (**Chapter 8**)
> Contact my Employer (**Chapter 9**)
> Contact Business Associates (**Chapter 10**)
> Funeral Arrangements (**Chapter 17**)

You must obtain certified copies of my death certificate. This is needed when dealing with insurance company claims and social security.

You will have to make arrangements for the disposition of my body. The information you will need for the death certificate can be found in **Chapter 4**, which contains my biographical information. You will also find other materials you will need there and in the zipper pouch contained in this portfolio. When requesting certified copies of the death certificate, ask for at least ten, as you will need these copies to complete various tasks. I recommend placing them in the pocket located in this section so that you will have all the necessary materials in one location.

If you have difficulty getting copies of my death certificate right away, you can request copies from the county in which I died. You can call the vital records office in that county, or you can even check online to see whether you can send a request via e-mail.

I am an organ donor, so please turn to **Chapter 15** to see the instructions for dealing with organ donation. You will find the necessary documents and contact information there.

My burial/cremation arrangement information can be found in **Chapter 16** in this portfolio. This section has the prior arrangements and my wishes contained therein. It will also contain information about where I wish to be buried or interred, and the documents related to prior arrangements for that site.

My funeral and memorial service arrangements and wishes can be found in **Chapter 17**.

Before you send out my obituary notice, found in **Chapter 18**, please make sure my house is secure. Often, these types of notices can entice thieves to rob a home because they think no one is there. (_____) has agreed to watch the house. His/her contact information is (_____).

Please contact the people in **Chapter 23** about my death or incapacitation. There are some people I do not wish for you to contact, and I have listed the reasons why in that same section of this portfolio.

It might be a good idea to make the arrangements listed in **Chapter 16** before contacting people so that you will have all the information to give them. This will save you time and energy, as I know these two things will be important right now.

My appointment calendar can be found (_____).

Please let those people with whom I have appointments know that they need to be cancelled. If you need further assistance, you may contact (_____).

Second Week

> Before a person becomes incapacitated, he or she should have done a durable power of attorney and an advance health care directive to let people of his or her choices. If they have not, there may need to be a time-consuming, expensive court process.
>
> Glenn A. Jarrett, Esq., CFP®, Jarrett Law Office, PLC

By this time, all the necessary burial arrangements have been completed, and more than likely, I will already be buried. Now is the time to deal with the will and other financial matters. I have tried hard to make this process as painless as possible. Money may be the last thing on your mind, but I want to make sure the ones I have left behind are taken care of, and that is why I have entrusted this important task to you.

My will can be found in **Chapter 19** and another copy can be located (_____).

During this week and the next couple of weeks, please contact all my banks, lending institutions, and other financial entities. The names and numbers can be found in **Chapter 19**.

In **Chapter 20**, I have all the insurance information you will need. It contains my policies and the contact information for the various companies and insurance agents. You will also need to cancel the following insurance policies (_____). information about these policies can be found in **Chapter 20**.

Information about my retirement and pensions can be found in **Chapter 23**. It has all the contact information and account numbers you will need.

Information about government benefits I am receiving can be found in **Chapter 23**. A copy of my social security card can be found in the zipper pouch in this portfolio.

You will need to contact all my service providers and doctors. Information about these providers can be found in **Chapter 12**.

My credit card account and debt companies will need to be notified of my death. All the most current information I could provide can be found in **Chapter 22**. There may be some credit cards and other accounts that may need to be closed immediately. Please keep my social security card and information safe, as this information can be used for fraud purposes. In six months to a year, I would suggest having my credit report pulled to see whether there is any illegal activity under my name, and this should be reported immediately.

Below, I am listing all my necessary passwords and what they are associated with. You may need these to handle my affairs.

Below, I have listed all the places where I have information or items stored securely. I have placed any safety deposit keys in (_____). Below are the locations that those keys are to be used.

The First Month and Beyond

By now, you will have handled my more immediate affairs. For the next month and beyond, I have listed the final items that need to be taken care of. Even though the instructions end here, my love for you and support are everlasting. Thank you for all that you have done for me.

In **Chapter 26**, you will find information about real estate I own, its location, and what is to be done with it.

In **Chapter 21**, you will locate information about all the vehicles I own or rent. You will find information about what is owed on them, where they are located, and what should be done with them.

If I have any other income or property, you can find out information about it in **Chapter 28**. You will find the locations, and information about what should be done with the property or income.

I have some memberships that need to be taken care of and cancelled. Information about these clubs can be found in **Chapter 11**.

If someone needs to complete a tax form for me this year, all my tax information can be located in **Chapter 27**, including past tax returns and documentation.

I hope that I have taken care of everything you will need. I know you will do everything brilliantly and that I have rightly placed my trust in you. I will leave you with this final thought:

Thank You and I Love You,

[Your Name]

CHAPTER 6

Your Children

The idea that might not be around to see your children grow up is a hard one to grasp. Of course, the odds are with you that you will see them through to college and beyond, but accidents and unfortunate events are never planned. This section represents what you would want to happen if the unexpected occurred.

Most people want to choose the person who takes care of their children, should they not be able to. Making the choice now reduces the possibility of a stranger working for the state making that decision, but there are no guarantees.

In rare situations, a court may not accept your choice for guardian. The candidate may have a criminal history or a record of abuse or neglect. It is important that you think about your decision thoroughly, and do a little research on your own. If there is a surviving parent, the court will look at him or her as the guardian before choosing someone else as caretaker.

Both you and the child's other parent should name the same person in each of your wills to prevent any sort of conflict. It will be hard enough for them to deal with your death without having to live with strangers and be fought over in court. Any disagreements you have with your child's other parent will be over, should one or both of you die.

> The guardians for your children should be close in age to you, does not have to be family, and should share your values. Provide enough financial assets to the guardians so that they may properly care for your children without being burdened. The beneficiary designations on life insurance, IRAs, and 401(k) accounts trump what your will says, so make sure they reflect your wishes (do not leave $200K to an ex-spouse, for example) And remember, minor children cannot inherit anything directly, so leave any inheritance for them to a trust for their benefit, even if it is testamentary. For younger couples, realize your spouse may remarry should you die. Leave your assets in a trust for their benefit during their lifetime, but have it ultimately go to your children when they die so you do not disinherit your children.
>
> James F. Seramba, Grey Oak Wealth Management

When considering a guardian for your child, here are some criteria:

- They must be an adult (18 years of age or older)

- They should have a close relationship with your child

- They should be mature and able to care for your child

- They should want to take care of your child

- You should consider the same guardian for all your children

- If they cannot be together, then each guardian should be close and allow access between the siblings

- They must be the best fit for each child's needs and wants

- Consider an alternative, should your first choice of guardian not work out

In addition to a guardian, you may also have to consider what is called a property manager. This person will manage any property or assets that are intended for a child. A minor child cannot own property, so there may be instances in which a manager may have to deal with a child's property until they are 18 years of age or older.

The property can be a trust, money willed to a child, or even physical property. Sometimes, the manager must ensure that some of the money is used for the care of a child until they can take an account over. The manager <u>will</u> decide how the money will be spent until the child can take over ownership of the property or assets. A parent may not automatically get the job as manager, even if they are the guardian of a child. If you want to name the parent, then you should do so in your will, and mention it in this section of your portfolio. If the other parent dies when you do, then you will want to name an alternate property manager. As in the case of a guardian, both parents should name the same manager in their wills.

Here are some criteria when picking a property manager:

- They must be good with money and investments

- They must be 18 years of age or older

- They should share your values when it comes to spending and investing money

- They should have the knowledge and experience of managing the types of assets that your child is entitled to

- You should name an alternative property manager, should your original choice not work out.

- They should be willing to take on the responsibility of managing your children's money

- They should not have a criminal or personal history of stealing or mismanaging money

It is important to note that even though you are naming the people you want as guardians and managers in this section of your portfolio, they must also be clearly stated in your will. Your portfolio is a quick reference guide, but legally, your choices must be named in your will.

In naming a property manager, you should consider setting up a trust with them as the trustee. This way, the person will not have to deal with the court; it will already have been taken care of, legally speaking. You should ask your financial advisor, attorney, or your bank about the best options concerning this.

I have included a document that you should fill out and file in this section of your portfolio. It will give anyone a quick reference of your choices and wishes concerning your children. It will also give the guardian important information concerning the care of your child.

> Try to keep your will simple, direct, and easy to understand. It is best to not try to control too much from the grave.
>
> Rodney M. Loesch JD CFP®, Loesch & Associates Inc.

My Children

In this section, I have described whom I want to take care of my children, if they are still minors, and how I want their care handled. Some of this information may be duplicated in my will, but here are the instructions and the necessary documents that the caregiver of my children will need in the event of my death or incapacitation.

Caregiver and Guardians

I have named whom I want to take care of each child below and listed their contact information.

Child #1

Child's Name :	DOB
Caregiver Name:	Caregiver Address:
Caregiver Phone Number:	Relationship to Child:
Alternate Caregiver Name:	Alternate Caregiver Address:
Alternate Caregiver Phone Number:	Relationship to Child:

Child #2

Child's Name :	DOB
Caregiver Name:	Caregiver Address:
Caregiver Phone Number:	Relationship to Child:
Alternate Caregiver Name:	Alternate Caregiver Address:
Alternate Caregiver Phone Number:	Relationship to Child:

Child #3

Child's Name :	DOB
Caregiver Name:	Caregiver Address:
Caregiver Phone Number:	Relationship to Child:
Alternate Caregiver Name:	Alternate Caregiver Address:
Alternate Caregiver Phone Number:	Relationship to Child:

Information about Children

Here is some additional information that will help in the care of my children.

Child #1

Name of Child's Provider	Contact Information
Doctor:	
Dentist	
Eye Doctor	
Specialist	
Other Necessary Information	
School	School Contact Information
Favorite Teacher	Favorite Toy
Health Conditions	Medications

Child #2

Name of Child's Provider	Contact Information
Doctor:	
Dentist	
Eye Doctor	
Specialist	

Other Necessary Information	
School	School Contact Information
Favorite Teacher	Favorite Toy
Health Conditions	Medications

Child #3

Name of Child's Provider	Contact Information
Doctor:	
Dentist	
Eye Doctor	
Specialist	
Other Necessary Information	
School	School Contact Information
Favorite Teacher	Favorite Toy
Health Conditions	Medications

In addition to the information you provide in the preceding document, you should also place the following items in the portfolio for each child, or at least make note of where the items can be found:

- Birth Certificates

- Social Security Cards

- Passports

- Immunization records

- School records

- Pictures

- Favorite stories

- Daily routines

- What you do when they are ill or scared

- How they like their hair (even who does their hair)

- Allergies (including food)

- Favorite foods (even recipes)

- Least favorite foods

- Fears and dreams

- A biography of each child's life, or just your favorite memories of them

You should include everything that will make their transition as easy as possible. You should also leave them with things to remember you by and that they will want to hold onto.

Children's Letters

Children's letters are similar to your letters to loved ones in your biography section. You can either write them a letter or make them a recording or video. Some parents even choose to make more than one letter to be opened at different stages in a child's life. This gives a child a feeling that their parent is still there, looking over them and giving them advice. While this may be hard to do, you likely want to leave everything you can for your children.

You can create letters for the following times:

- High School

- Special birthdays

- Graduation

- First car/license

- Dating

- Heart broken

- Marriage

- First child

- College

- First job

- Your hopes and dreams for them

- Advice about various subjects in life

CHAPTER 7

Care of Others

You may have adult dependents that you are responsible for, or people you chose to look in on and take care of. Family and friends may not know anything about these people, and since they rely on you, it is important to record information about them in this section so others can pick up the responsibility and not leave these people uncared for.

In this section, you need to name who these people are, where they are, and how they should be taken care of should you become incapacitated or die. It is a good idea to talk to others about taking over your responsibilities before you are in a situation in which you cannot make these arrangements. Let them know you are naming them in your portfolio and, if needed, in your will. The next page is a document you should fill out and place in this section of your portfolio.

Information about Adults who Rely on Me

This is a list of people I care for in various functions. Please help make sure they are cared for, and contact the person I have named as a caregiver.

Name:	Address:
Phone Number:	
DOB	My Relationship to the Person:
Type of Care I Provide:	
Contact Information of Appointed Caregiver:	

Name:	Address:
Phone Number:	
DOB	My Relationship to the Person:
Type of Care I Provide:	
Contact Information of Appointed Caregiver:	

Name:	Address:
Phone Number:	
DOB	My Relationship to the Person:
Type of Care I Provide:	
Contact Information of Appointed Caregiver:	

Additional Caregivers

The following is a list of people who also provide care for the individuals listed above.

Person's Name	Caregiver's Contact Information	Relationship to Person	Type of Care They Provide

If there is any information that will help in the care of the people you name in the document, you should place it in this section. Here is a list of examples:

- Doctor information

- Social security number

- Nutrition needs

- Medications they are taking

- A schedule or calendar of appointments

- Health care issues

- Social security benefit information

- Debts you pay for them

- Bank account information

- Legal guardianship or power of attorney documents

- Lists of their relatives' contact information

CHAPTER 8

Your Pets

You may have pets, or even livestock, that you need to make arrangements for. It is important that you make these arrangements as soon as possible, and then list those arrangements in your portfolio and will. You should prepare the person whom you are making the new owner of your favorite cat or dog, or whom you need to take over your farm and livestock. You should have alternative caregivers listed in case your first choice cannot care for your pets at the time of your death or incapacitation.

Never assume that others know what your wishes are concerning your pets. Make sure your wishes are known, and that you are placing them in the appropriate section of your portfolio. If you do not have anyone who can care for your pets, you can contact your local Humane Society about arrangements. You can request a "Providing for Your Pet's Future Without You" kit by calling the Humane Society at 202-452-1100, or by visiting **http://www.hsus.org/pets/pet_care/providing_for_your_pets_future_without_you**.

In the appendix you can find a list of veterinary schools that may be able to care for your pets.

Pet Care Instructions

The following is a list of people who also provide care for the individuals listed above.

Pet's name, species, and identifying marks	Location of Animal	Food and Water Regimen

Health and other care instructions	Person whom I name to care for my pet and their contact information	Veterinarian's name and number

You may also wish to create a trust for your pet so they will be taken care of beyond your life. You should contact your attorney about how to set this up. Make sure you include this information in your portfolio and will.

Other items you may wish to include in your portfolio include:

- Type of food or treats your pet loves

- Your pet's favorite toy or place to sleep

- Your pet's schedule of walking

- Your pet's temperament

- Your pet's pedigree papers

- Immunization records, including rabies vaccines

- Information about a pet electronic chip implant

- Your pet's medical history

- Pet's allergies

CHAPTER 9

Employment

> You worked 18 years for Uncle Sam and 32 years for yourself.
> With estate taxes, it increases to 31 years, or 62 percent of your
> working life — just to pay taxes.
>
> Mike Kilbourn, Kilbourn Associates

You will want to have your employment information to help in the
process of settling your estate. You should include important phone
numbers and contacts. There may be some crossover in the section
of your portfolio, especially in the areas of pensions, insurance, and
benefits. Also include any retirement information and account numbers
in the section.

> The IRS sheds no tears for those who don't plan.
>
> Mike Kilbourn, Kilbourn Associates

The next page is a document that you may wish to fill out and have in
the beginning of the employment section in your portfolio. It has places
to enter all your important employment information.

Employment Information

Upon my incapacitation or death, please contact my current employers, below. You should ask about any benefits, pensions, or insurance that I may have, but may have failed to record here. Please determine whether there are any unpaid wages or commissions, expense reimbursements, or bonuses that may be due to my estate.

Employer's Contact Information	Current Benefits	
	My Position	
	Start Date	
	Ownership Interest	❑ Yes (%) ❑ No
Employer's Contact Information	Current Benefits	
	My Position	
	Start Date	
	Ownership Interest	❑ Yes (%) ❑ No

Previous Jobs (This section needs only to be filled out if you receive benefits from that company.)

Employer's Contact Information	Current Benefits	
	My Position	
	Start Date	End Employment Date
	Ownership Interest	❑ Yes (%) ❑ No

Employer's Contact Information	Current Benefits	
	My Position	
	Start Date	End Employment Date
	Ownership Interest	❑ Yes (%) ❑ No

Employer's Contact Information	Current Benefits	
	My Position	
	Start Date	End Employment Date
	Ownership Interest	❏ Yes (%) ❏ No

In this section, you may want to have copies of your wage verification, a description of your job, any raises, descriptions of benefits, retirement account numbers, locations of your retirement accounts, and any other documents that are relevant to your job and job history.

CHAPTER 10

Business Ownership

If a person has a business, he or she should have a business succession plan in place and take steps to insure the business won't be stuck in limbo if the person dies or becomes disabled. There should be a person in place who can run the business. This can be the power of attorney agent in the event of disability, the executor in the will, or the trustee of a living trust. Key employees can play a part, too. This will depend in part on how the business is structured (sole proprietorship vs. LLC vs. corporation).

Glenn A. Jarrett, Esq., CFP®, Jarrett Law Office, PLC

Sell it before the person dies so it's not caught up in administration. See an attorney about taking advantage of all of the specialized planning for businesses, such as trusts, giving, and loaning. There are a myriad of ways that the taxes can be reduced on small businesses, all of which take the guidance of a professional.

Kim Allen-Niesen , Retired Estate Planning Attorney

A person owning a business must first decide what he wants to happen if he becomes incapacitated or dies. If you have children who want to go into the business, you must work out an estate plan that is fair to all of the children; this can be especially difficult if all of them are not involved in the business.

Joseph H. Gruner, Gaines Gruner Ponzini & Novick, LLC

This section may be optional for those who do not own a business. Also, if you only own stock or stock options in a company, you too may skip this chapter. You can add that information under the bank accounts section or in the "other income" section of your portfolio. If, however, you are a business owner, then you should take your time, as your business may constitute the bulk of your estate.

There are four pages of documents that I have added for you to fill out and have prominently displayed in the front of this section. It will contain all the key information that your loved ones will need to know about your business. Your wishes about your business will also be spelled out in the will, but this section can provide a quick reference guide, as well as the necessary documents needed to run your company.

You need to determine how much of the business you own. If you have partners, you need to disclose who they are and what they are responsible for in the company. You will also need to think about how the business will continue after your death, and who will take on your shares and responsibilities. You may wish to transfer your interest in the company or have it sold with the assets to be distributed to your loved ones as named in your will. If you do not have all your important business records in your portfolio, you need to make a note in this section what those documents are and where they can be located.

There are different types of business that you may own. Below are descriptions of different structures and how you may choose to handle each in your portfolio and will.

- **Sole Proprietorship:** As you are the only owner in this type of structure, it will cease to exist when you do. You may choose to give the assets to someone or for it to be sold upon your death.

- **Partnership:** In this type of situation, you may have a few different options. The company may be taken over by your partner, or he or she may buy your interests out in the company. The company may dissolve completely if your partner decides not to continue the business after you are gone.

- **Limited Liability Company (LLC):** In the case of an LLC, the company will dissolve if one of the owners dies. There is an exception to this, if it is clearly written in the bylaws or charter of the LLC.

- **Corporation:** In this type of business structure, the business is a legal entity in and of itself. It is separated from the individuals involved in the corporation. If someone dies, it will not have a legal affect on the company. The shares that you own may be passed to your heirs or bought out by the corporation.

It is important for you to decide what is to be done with your company or your shares in a company. If you want your heirs to continue your company, you must devise a plan for them to take over. Consider whether they have ever run a company before, or have experience in your company or type of business.

> My advice for business owners is to have a buy-sell in place for both death and disability that is air-tight. Have a succession plan in place and well know, groom your successor(s) early, develop an enterprise that can continue on, even after you are not there, so you are not irreplaceable, and have key man insurance on yourself.
>
> James F. Seramba, Grey Oak Wealth Management

> The person should have a clear succession plan or should think about selling the business prior to becoming too old. The succession plan can be as simple as having the children take over, but often, the succession plan will involve having stock in the business purchased by key employees. These can all look different, but often, the business represents a significant portion of the business owner's wealth. Anytime there is a transfer to children, the business owner is left at the mercy of the children, and the risk that they may ruin the business.
>
> Stephen L. Smith, Esq., Horack, Talley, Pharr & Lowndes, P.A.

There are some places you can access for help in preparing your company and making sound decisions about what will happen upon your death or incapacitation.

- Small Business Association (**www.sba.gov**) has considerable information about small business, along with articles, forms, links, and advice. The SBA also sponsors **www.Businesslaw.gov**, which has suggestions about what to do with your company and how to plan for the future.

- The Service Corps of Retired Executives can be accessed at **www.score.org**, or you can call them at 800-634-0245. This organization provides both over-the-phone and in-person assistance and counseling about your business options. This is a free service.

- You may access the CCH Business Owner's Toolkit at **www.toolkit.com/**. This kit contains advice on a number of financial, legal, and tax issues that your small business may face.

> A well-written business plan and business succession plan is important in closely held businesses. In addition, life insurance policies can help family members continue your business when you are no longer around to take care of it.
>
> Gabriel Cheong, Esq., Infinity Law Group LLC

If you intend to have your heirs take over your company, you may want to speak with them about it and begin to teach them how to run the company. You are never too young to start the process. You may even find that they do not want to take over when you are gone, which may force you to change your plans about the future of your company beyond your passing.

Most of the documents at the end of this chapter are self-explanatory, but there are few sections that may bear explanation so that you will enter the information correctly.

The first section is a general description of your business. It provides information about the location of your business and what is involved in its operation. It will also include all the locations of subsidiary offices and branches. It is important that you record every office that is associated with your business, and its location.

The next section deals with the ownership of your company. It describes the following:

- Who the owners are

- Contact information for the owners

- Job title of each owner and description of what they do

- How much of the company each owner has interests or shares in

- Documents related to the ownership and structure of the company (if they are not attached to this section of the book, the location of those documents should be noted here)

The next section is the disposition of the company, which refers to what should happen to the company upon your death or incapacitation. If you only have a share or interest in the company, then you should also describe how you want your interest in the company handled, whether it should be sold, liquidated, or handed down. The next section deals with key people involved with the company. It should have their contact information and how they are involved.

If there are any documents related to the disposition of your company, then you should either attach them to this section of the portfolio or record where those documents can be found.

The next section of the document deals with any employees that you may have hired in the company. It will contain a list of employees and their contact information. This section will also have information about pay and benefits of the employees, as well as how those employees should be handled in the disposition of the company.

It is a good idea to have your business tax information included in your portfolio. You should have your current year's information, as well as the prior year's information and forms. Having these documents either attached or their location mentioned on the document will save someone considerable time and money.

The last part of the document deals with the assets and liabilities associated with your company. You should list all these and have documents or their location listed on the document. This is an important section if someone is taking over the company or if you plan for the company to be liquidated.

> Business owners have added complexities involved in handling their estates. They must find the most advantageous way to pass what often is their biggest asset, their business. Typically, this is done through business succession planning and often takes the shape of either a buy-sell agreement or a family succession plan.
>
> Christopher J. Berry, Esq., Witzke Berry PLLC

The information contained in this section relates to my business interests. Specifically, it deals with information about whom to contact in the event of my death or if I should become incapacitated. This information can also be used to help you manage or sell my business interests.

Current Business Interests

These are businesses I currently own or have interest in.

Name and Location

Name of Business	Location and Telephone of Business	Where to find documents related to business

Ownership

Who Owns the Business	Address and Phone Number of Owner	Owner's Job Title or Position	What Percentage They Own

These are businesses I currently own or have interest in.

Name and Location

Directions Concerning Disposition of Entire Business			
Directions Concerning My Interest			
Contact Information for Key Individuals			
Name	Position	Contact Information	Their Role in Business
Disposition Documents			
Tax ID Number			
State ID Number			

Employees

This section deals with the people who are key in keeping the business running.

Employee Name	Type of agreement they have with company	Benefits	Contact Information

Business Taxes

Tax Record Information

Current-Year Records	Location of Documents
	Who is Responsible for documents
Prior-Year Records	Location of Documents
	Who is Responsible for documents

Assets and Liabilities

This section lists assets and liabilities. This information is intended to help manage, transfer, or sell the business.

Assets

Description of Particular Asset	Current Location of Asset	Value of Asset	Contact Name and Information	Location of Asset Documents

Liabilities

Description of Particular Asset	Current Location of Asset	Value of Asset	Contact Name and Information	Location of Asset Documents

Prior Business Interests

This section deals with my investments, rights, and responsibilities in businesses I have owned in the past, but any such investments, rights, and responsibilities have been fully resolved and terminated. In these businesses, there should be no additional expenses that will be incurred and no income collected. This information is for reference purposes in the event that any future claims arise.

Business Name	Location of Business	Location of Ownership and Dissolution Documents	Date Company Responsibility was Resolved
Contact Information			

Business Name	Location of Business	Location of Ownership and Dissolution Documents	Date Company Responsibility was Resolved
Contact Information			

Business Name	Location of Business	Location of Ownership and Dissolution Documents	Date Company Responsibility was Resolved
Contact Information			

All of the forms can be copied for each business in which interest is owned. You can further separate this larger section into smaller sections to organize each separate business to reduce confusion. Label everything carefully and ensure that any documents not contained in your portfolio are noted in your portfolio along with their locations.

In organizing your estate, list account access information (passwords and PINS) and the contact information for the important people and professionals in your life (such as family, friends, doctors, lawyers, and tax professionals).

Jennifer R. Lewis Kannegieter, Attorney at Law

CHAPTER 11

Clubs and Other Organizations

> Two things are guaranteed, death and taxes. If you were to flip a coin 1,000 times, statistically, you could expect about half of the flips to be heads. But, you don't get 1,000 chances to make it come out heads, and there is every bit as much chance that your one flip will come out tails. You are going to die; so, why not plan?
>
> Mike Kilbourn, Kilbourn Associates

There are many different organizations you may belong to. Some of the memberships will terminate upon your death, while others may be passed on to your spouse or children. Like everything else you include in your portfolio, it is important that you include as much information as possible, and if you cannot fit it into the portfolio, make a note about where it can be located.

Below are some of the more common types of organizations and examples of each.

Type of Organizations

Professional Organizations

- Business types can include Chamber of Commerce or the

Jaycees. These types of organizations help promote your business.

- Professional types include organizations such as the American Medical Association, Medical Boards, American Farm Bureau, or even Bridal Association of America. These types of organizations are designed to help you professionally through networking and certifications.

- Trade Unions exist in different parts of the United States. Examples of these types of organizations are Teamsters, United Steel Workers of America, United Farm Workers, and United Auto Workers. These types of organizations offer many benefits for workers in certain types of industries. They may even offer benefit packages.

- Veteran's organizations can include Veterans of Foreign Wars or the American Legion. You can find a list of other types of these organizations at the Department of Veteran Affairs, at **www1.va.gov/vso**. These organizations help veterans of every branch from every war. These can help families plan for burial arrangements and have information about memorials and places you can be buried.

- Civic Rights organizations also fit under this category. Some examples of these types of organizations are the American Civil Liberties Union, League of Women Voters, and the National Rifle Association. These membership organizations offer benefits to their members, such as newsletters, magazines, legal assistance, and a variety of specialized services, depending on the particular organization.

Most professional organization memberships end when a person dies.

Some offer benefits to their survivors. It is a good idea to read your membership information, because your family may be entitled to certain benefits that you are not aware of.

Fraternal Organizations

These types of organizations have specialized membership, but often do public and charitable works, both locally and internationally. These types of organizations include:

- Moose Lodge
- Eastern Star
- Lions Club International
- Rotary Club
- Kiwanis Club
- Freemason Lodges
- Job's Daughters

These clubs sometimes offer benefits to families after you pass away. If nothing else, they can provide support to a family during their time of need. Some organizations can help with funeral arrangements and may even have specialized burial ceremonies and memorials. Sometimes, membership in a particular fraternal organization entitles your children to a place in the same or an associated organization. An example is Job's Daughters and the Freemasons. In order to be a member of Job's Daughters, you must be the daughter of a Master Mason, which is a person who has achieved the highest rank in a Freemason Lodge. Eastern Star is the sister organization to the Freemasons.

In addition to member information, many of these fraternal organizations have regalia that you may want to pass down. Keep these items are together in a secure place, like a safety deposit box. These are important pieces that can help pass down your heritage to the next generation.

Educational Membership Organizations

These types of organizations are usually associated with colleges and institutions of higher learning. Even after a person has graduated, they are still a part of these national and international organizations. These types of organizations include:

- Alumni Association

- Honor Societies

- Fraternities

- Sororities

- Special Interest Fraternities

These types of organizations are similar to fraternal organizations in that they often do public and charitable works. They often give back to the particular school they are associated with. These organizations provide networks for people in their professional lives beyond college. You may want to check with your particular educational organization, as they sometimes provide automatic admission for your children when they go to college because you were a member.

As with fraternal organizations, there is often regalia and photos that are associated with these types of organizations. Make sure you place these items together and make a note in this section of your portfolio on where they can be located.

Social Clubs

There are a few different types of clubs that fit into this category. The purpose of these types of clubs is to have fun and to socialize. They often have common interests, and occasionally, they may help raise money for different charitable pursuits.

- Cultural Clubs are those that contain people of similar background s or ethnicities. Some examples are the Urban League, the Sons of Poland, the National Association for the Advancement of Colored People, and the Italian Club.

- There are certain clubs that are formed because of people's lineage, such as the Daughters of the Revolution, Sons of Confederate Veterans, or the Mayflower Society. To be a member of these clubs, you must be able to prove your lineage. Your children, obviously, would also be eligible members of these organizations, so it is important to pass down proof of your lineage.

Recreational Organizations

These are organizations that have some sort of recreational or athletic theme. These types of organizations include:

- Sports related clubs, such as gyms, spas, or athletic teams.

- Artistic clubs, such as quilting, lapidary, writing, or reading clubs. These may not be organized clubs, but may exist as small groups of friends.

- Clubs that are formed around hobbies, such as coin collecting, wine tasting, bird watching, or geocaching (which involves looking for hidden treasures using portable global positioning satellite units).

- Youth groups, which do activities to help children in a variety of mediums. Examples of these types of clubs are the boy scouts, the girl scouts, the Boys and Girls Club of America, and 4-H.

Religious and Spiritual Organizations

These are groups you may be affiliated with that are religious or spiritual in nature. These are groups that are beyond your membership in a church congregation. Examples of these types of groups include:

- Bible study groups (or any other type of religious study group)

- Meditation group

- Drumming circle

- Church related activity groups

- Church choir

This is meant as a basic list, but there are many other types of religious and spiritual groups. There are also healing types of groups that sometimes have a spiritual component, and sometimes do not, including:

- Self-help groups

- Twelve-step programs

- Divorce groups

- Weight Watchers

- Cancer survivors groups

Charitable Organizations

These types of organizations have the sole purpose to help fund specific causes. Most of these organizations ask for donations to keep working at a particular cause. It is not unusual for someone to make a charitable organization the beneficiary to their will. This is more often the case if the person has no children to leave their estate to. These types of organizations can be broken down into five main categories.

1. Civic organizations are aimed toward the needs of the local community. Friends of the Library or groups dedicated to creating a park are good examples of these types of groups.

2. Needy groups are those groups whose purpose is to help those less fortunate and unable to pay for things, such as food and medical care. Soup kitchens and free clinics fall under this type of organization.

3. Environmental groups include those dedicated to helping save the earth and its inhabitants in a variety of different ways. Greenpeace, Nature Conservancy, and Sierra Club are types of clubs dedicated to the environment.

4. Arts groups support art in its many forms, such as music, dance, drama, and visual arts. There are a number of different local and national endowments for the arts that fall into this category of charitable organization.

5. There are many different faith-based and religious organizations that do a number of local and international deeds to help the homeless, hungry, and destitute.

Consumer-Based Memberships

There are many different corporations, both large and small, that have some sort of membership program. These programs serve a few purposes. First, they provide consumers with free merchandise or services or a discount on those products and services. These memberships allow companies to track who is buying their product and allows them to give shoppers an incentive to continue to buy their product or service.

- Grocery store memberships can allow you discounts at the

register, enter you into contests and sweepstakes, and even accumulate points for later purchases.

- Cumulative memberships are the types that allow you to purchase products and services after you have accumulated enough points. Examples of these are frequent flyer programs and even restaurants.

- Some retail stores have memberships that need to be renewed yearly. These memberships allow you access to their store, which promises you discounts on products. Costco and Sam's are examples of these types of memberships. You may want to pay close attention to these because they may have automatic drafts at renewal time.

- There are companies that have memberships that allow you access to certain privileges. These are usually on a yearly membership cycle and, as with retail stores, dues may automatically be drafted from your bank account. Be sure to note this in your portfolio.

Community Memberships

These are memberships to local clubs or associations in your neighborhood or community. These types of memberships may have fees attached to them, and there may be contracts involved that need to be included in your portfolio. Following are some examples of community memberships.

- Housing or building associations may regulate your condominium or housing development. There is often a fee charged monthly or annually. These types of associations can be passed down along with your home, but you need to make sure all the details and beneficiaries are worked out and that you include that information in your portfolio.

- Country Clubs and golf memberships are another type of membership that you need to be aware of. In some cases, these can be handed down. Just make sure you include financial information, locations of the clubs, and when dues are owed.

Subscriptions

You may not think of these as strictly memberships, but in many ways, subscriptions work the same as other types of memberships. You should include a list of different subscriptions, how often a product arrives, what the cost is, and when renewal is due. Many subscriptions can be redirected to someone else until they run out, so include contact information for each company, or at least how someone can go about a change of address. Indicate how you usually pay for these subscriptions, as they can be renewed automatically through a bank account or credit card.

- Newspapers and magazines can come daily, weekly, monthly, bimonthly, or even annually. Make sure you include where each of these is being delivered.

- Product-of-the-month clubs are common. These can involve wine, food, chocolate, or even pajamas. These are sometimes given as gifts, but like other types of subscriptions, can be redirected.

There may be less formal but equally important memberships you are associated with. If you get a regular delivery of certain types of goods or food, you will want to include this in your memberships section. Examples may be a food co-op or food company, such as Schwan's. Include the delivery schedule, contact information, and payment schedule.

For your loved ones, finding and cancelling all your memberships can be frustrating and time consuming. It may not seem as important as the location of your stock portfolio, but it can be more tedious for those who have to deal with it. If a particular membership automatically drafts payments from your account, it is especially important to stop the membership and the payments.

Survivor Benefits

As I have mentioned throughout this chapter, some memberships can be transferred to your loved ones. Some of the more common types of memberships that can be passed down are:

- Consumer-based memberships

- Subscriptions to periodicals

- Transferable services in which all the dues are paid

One membership that you should be focused on should be frequent flyer programs, due to the value of such memberships. Each airline may handle these memberships differently, so you need to pay close attention to the details in your membership materials. If you do not wish to transfer your points to your beneficiaries, you can donate them to charitable organizations, such as:

- Special Olympics — These provide transportation for participants to travel to Special Olympics events where they may not have otherwise been able to attend.

- The American Red Cross miles that are donated are used to help volunteers respond to a disaster and provide relief for those in need.

- Operation Hero Miles is an organization that helps troops

stationed overseas to get home on emergency leave. These miles also allow family members to fly to a hospital where a wounded soldier is recovering.

You may also have the option of selling or trading your air miles. You must check with each individual airline you have frequent air miles programs with for details. You can sometimes use the miles to purchase items such as tickets to a concert or athletic event.

It is a good idea to contact the companies in which you hold memberships. Talk with them about what paperwork and procedures need to be completed should you become incapacitated or die. You might be able to have the paperwork available in your portfolio. Some companies will even provide refunds of dues in the event of death or incapacitation. You need to find out what the policies are and include them along with what you have paid on a particular membership.

You can include membership documents and certificates in your portfolio. You can place membership cards in a zippered bag in the portfolio, along with other smaller items. Again, keep all this information updated.

The form below should be included in the membership portion of your portfolio. It can also be found on the CD-ROM attached to this book. It will include information about all your memberships and contact information for the organizations to which you belong.

Memberships

In this section, I have placed lists of all the clubs, groups, programs, subscriptions, and organizations that I belong to. This information can be used should I become incapacitated or upon my death. You should cancel all necessary memberships and make note of those that will transfer to others. You should also contact the necessary companies about a change of address, especially for subscriptions.

Name of Organization	Dues Paid On
	Amount of Dues
Necessary Contact Information	Membership Number
What to do with Membership	

Name of Organization	Dues Paid On
	Amount of Dues
Necessary Contact Information	Membership Number
What to do with Membership	

Name of Organization	Dues Paid On
	Amount of Dues
Necessary Contact Information	Membership Number
What to do with Membership	

CHAPTER 12

List of Service Providers

There are many people who provide services in your life, from doctors and dentists, to counselors and acupuncturists. There are even people who cut your hair, trim the hedges, service your car, and even do your nails. Many of these providers have you penciled into their appointment calendar for your next appointment. If you are incapacitated or die, they need to be notified. If there is an unsettled account with these providers, it must be taken care of. Some who provide services such as lawn care may need to be continued with, just the billing arrangements changed.

You should include each of these providers in this section of your portfolio. All their contact information, what they charge, how often they provide a service, and any contracts with these providers should be stored in this section.

While it may not be practical to keep every current appointment in your portfolio, you should note where this information can be located, such as your calendar or computer files. If you have an outstanding bill with a particular provider, you should include this information, or at least indicate where this information can be located. You should include additional information about services that will continue or information that your loved ones may need to know about. A common example is to make a note that the maid has a set of keys to your house.

Here are some lists of typical professional providers that you may use.

Professional Service Providers

Medical Services		
Family Doctor	Specialists	Alternative Health Provider
Chiropractor	Massage Therapist	Physical Therapy
Speech Therapy	Occupational Therapy	Chemotherapy

Dental Services		
Family Dentist	Orthodontist	Dental Specialist

Vision Services		
Optometrist	Ophthalmologist	Eye Specialist

Hearing Services	
Audiologist	Hearing Aid Specialist

Mental Health Services		
Social Worker	Psychiatrist	Psychologist
Counselor	Spiritual Counselor	

Grooming Services		
Hair Stylist	Nail Specialist	Tanning Bed Operator

Day-to-Day Services	
Assisted Shopping	Meal Preparation
Medical Transportation	Appointment Driver

Home Services	
Lawn Specialist	Landscaper
Gardener	Odd Jobs Person
Maintenance Services	Pool and Spa Services
Pest Control Services	Maid Service
Piano Tuner	Private Lessons
Computer Support and Maintenance	

Vehicle Service Providers		
Mechanic	Car Detailer	Car Maintenance Services

The following forms are to be used in your portfolio. You should gather all the material about all the providers in your life and their contact information. You will also be able to find this form on the CD-ROM attached to this book. The forms are separated into two categories — medical and other providers.

Professional Providers

You will find lists of health care providers and other professional providers I use. You will find information on who they are, how often I use them, payment schedule, and contact information. You will need to cancel many services, and others will need to be continued. You will find all the necessary documents and contracts in this section of my portfolio.

Medical Providers

Name and Contact Information	Type of Care and Location	Frequency of Visits	Billing Instructions	Other Notes

Other Service Providers

Name and Contact Information	Type of Care and Location	Billing Arrangement	What to do about Service	Other Notes

CHAPTER 13

Life Support Information

Medical directives are, in my opinion, essential. They give someone you trust the power to make medical decisions for you if you are not able to. They also remove all of the guess work as to what kind of care and treatment you desire in certain situations and make the decisions for your loved ones much easier. For example, if you do not want to be placed on a respirator, it would be suggested that you take all legal steps necessary in your state to make sure your wishes are carried out and that you do not leave that decision to your family members. Any decision made by family members will just add more stress and tension to an already tense and stressful situation. Any decision will be second-guessed for years to come. If you leave specific instructions, your loved ones will at least take solace in the fact that they are doing exactly what you had wished.

Steven J. Maffei, Attorney at Law

The key thing is to have financial and health care powers of attorney in place, which in North Carolina are durable so they last past incompetency and incapacity. This allows the person's affairs to be handled and their health care wishes to be carried out, even though they are not capable of acting themselves.

Stephen L. Smith, Esq., Horack, Talley, Pharr & Lowndes, P.A.

> I believe a medical directive is a very kind thing to do for your health care agent (HCA, the one you want to make medical decisions for you — or who is arbitrarily assigned if you don't state your wishes). You can state the latitude your HCA has in making decisions, when you want end-of-life decisions to be made, what medical procedures you would permit, and how difficult medical choices are made. In essence, you make medical decisions for yourself just as you would if you were capable, and give guidance on how other decisions are made.
>
> David M. Williams, CFP®

This book is not only for situations in which you may pass away, but it is also for situations in which you could become incapacitated, possibly due to an injury or disease. Whatever the reason, you would not be able to handle your own affairs any further. Following this section will ensure that your wishes and thoughts concerning your care are known and followed.

It is important that you have the necessary documents signed and in a place people can find them in case of an emergency. If certain documents are not immediately available, medical professionals will do whatever they need to sustain your life indefinitely, which is why it is imperative that you take care of your medical directives.

There are two different documents that you will need to be concerned with and make sure you have, not only in your portfolio, but easily accessible in your home, work, and vehicles.

> Medical directives are absolutely a must. A family should not be put through the extra anguish brought on by a person not responsibly preparing medical directives.
>
> Jane S Eddy, ChFC, CLU

I think this is by far the most important legal document a person can make if they have specific needs and wants. This is the document that prevents someone from being on life support for extended periods of time, existing by machine. Some people want every technological advantage to prolong their lives, and others want nothing to do with it. If you have an opinion, the Living Will is the paramount directive you need. Also, I feel that this is an extremely valuable document in terms of taking the guilt and remorse away from your loved ones, if they should have to decide when to terminate life support. By giving them clear terms as to when you want to suspend life support, you remove from their conscience the feelings of doubt. It is truly the best gift you can give to your loved ones, far beyond any amount of money.

David T. Pisarra, Esq.

Health Care Declaration

The first directive is called a declaration. This document is a statement directly to any medical personnel explaining what you do and do not want in relation to medical care and procedures. You should be as detailed as possible concerning what your wishes are, should you become unable to express them directly. There are some areas that you will want to consider when creating a health care declaration. Each state has certain forms that you will need for your health care declaration, so you should check with your attorney or talk to someone at your local hospital about where you can locate the necessary forms. You may also want to ask them where they will look for your medical directive forms in case of an emergency.

The first area to consider is life prolonging procedures and treatments. These procedures are for the purpose of keeping your body alive for as long as possible. This can mean that you could be in a permanent coma, in which case they would sustain your body, whether there was any hope of your regaining consciousness or not. Some of the procedures that could be involved are a respirator, the administration of medications and antibiotics, surgery, dialysis, or cardiopulmonary resuscitation (CPR). Whether a blessing or a curse, medical science can keep your body and tissues alive indefinitely.

In your declaration, you can state that you do not want any life saving procedures or you can state which ones are acceptable and which ones are not. If you do not wish to be revived, there is what is called a Do Not Resuscitate (DNR). This order lets medical professionals know not to try to revive you or administer CPR. This order is often in place for people who are near death. You can have a bracelet or medical alert jewelry that will have DNR on it, but you still need to have your documentation nearby. Make sure that your local hospital and your doctor have copies of your medical directive documents.

Another area to consider on a declaration is whether you would want food and drink administered if you were incapacitated. If you are near death or permanently unconscious, you need to decide whether you want nutrition and hydration. Unless you have a declaration that states otherwise, medical personnel will give you nutrition through your veins and a nasal gastric tube to keep your body alive and functioning.

Your body can last years with this sort of hydration and nutrition, even if there is no hope of you regaining consciousness. If you make a statement that you do not want this type of care, they will stop these procedures and your body will die naturally. A doctor would give your body medications to ease any discomfort.

Medications to ease pain and discomfort are areas to consider adding to your health care declaration. The assumption is that regardless of whether you want long-term care, you would want care to keep your body comfortable. Sometimes referred to as palliative care, medications to keep your body comfortable can be administered until your body naturally dies.

> Durable powers of attorneys and any trust documents should contain an incapacity clause to ensure that they will continue to be legal and effective when you need them the most. Estate planning documents not only tell people where your things should go after you pass away, but a good estate plan will help you while you're still alive.
>
> Gabriel Cheong, Esq., Infinity Law Group LLC

Power of Attorney

A durable power of attorney gives a designated health care agent (sometimes referred to as a medical proxy) power over your affairs. This gives them the power to make decisions when you cannot make those decisions for yourself. You can place limits on them if you choose, or give them complete power over your health care.

The health care agent can make decisions about the following areas:

- They can consent to or refuse treatment being administered to you. There may be limits to this in areas of extreme psychosis or terminating a pregnancy early.

- They can decide about who gives you medical care. They can fire a medical person, if they deem it necessary, and hire someone else.

- They can decide where you receive medical treatment.

- They can visit you any time in a facility, even when others may be restricted.

- They can have access to your personal and medical records.

- They can go to court in matters of obtaining or sustaining specific medical treatments.

- In most areas, they will be in charge of the disposition of your body. You need to let this person know where they can locate your portfolio and other necessary documents.

- They can be responsible for notifying clergy about your condition and allowing them to perform certain religious ceremonies on your behalf.

You should trust 100 percent your medical proxy 100 percent. If you have the slightest doubt that they will follow your wishes, you should either not pick that person as your proxy or you should have another person be co-proxy. Remember that your proxy will speak for you in regards to medical decisions when you cannot speak for yourself, so you want this person to have the same values as you do. For this reason, sometimes a close family member is not the best choice because they might have a personal and emotional attachment to you being alive, while it might not be your wish to stay alive by artificial means. These conflicts should be considered before choosing a proxy.

Gabriel Cheong, Esq., Infinity Law Group LLC

My advice for medical directives is to make sure to let family members know they exist and are readily available. Have the person discuss their desires with their physicians ahead of time as well.

James F. Seramba, Grey Oak Wealth Management

In a perfect world, you would have one person handle your financial affairs as well as your health care decisions and your health care power of attorney. However, we have often found that a person who may be a good choice as far as acting as your agent under a health care power of attorney does not necessarily have good financial sense (so that you would not necessarily want them acting under a financial power of attorney), and so you may end up with more than one person acting, depending on the strengths of the various people.

Stephen L. Smith, Esq., Horack, Talley, Pharr & Lowndes, P.A.

An agent cannot override your wishes, as long as you have them clearly stated. That is why the creation of and the access to your portfolio are imperative. Having a copy of your portfolio and allowing someone else to have access to it is not a bad idea either.

Even if you have a power of attorney granted to an agent, you should also have a health care declaration. This declaration helps your agent know what your wishes are so that they can make sure that the declaration is followed.

A medical professional can refuse to honor the wishes of your agent or the statements in your declaration. This can occur if it goes against the conscience of the provider, violates the policies of the health care institution, or causes a problem in standard health care practice. If this occurs, they must notify you or your agent. Your agent then has the option to hire a new provider or move you to another institution. In some states, if a health care provider refuses to honor the wishes of the patient or their agent, they can be held legally and financially liable.

If you are having difficulty finding the appropriate forms for a Power of Attorney or health care declaration, here is a list of suggested places to ask for help:

- Senior centers

- Long-term care facilities

- Hospital

- Health care provider

- Medical association in your state

- Hospice

A health agent is also referred to as a durable power of attorney. He or she will only have control while you are incapacitated. If you are able to make decisions, then he or she has no power over medical decisions.

> Medical directives or living wills are a necessity. After the Terry Shiavo incident, everyone should see the importance of executing a health care proxy and living will. Because in some states, a living will is not binding and your health care proxy can make decisions on your behalf despite your wishes, it is still important to have a living will. It is an instrument that guides your proxy or doctors and articulates your wishes when you do not have the ability to communicate them.
>
> **Gabriel Cheong, Esq., Infinity Law Group LLC**

Below are some forms that you may wish to fill out and place in your portfolio. Again, make sure that these same forms can be easily accessible in other areas. If an ambulance arrives on the scene of an accident, they will do everything they can to revive you and sustain your life. They may look in your glove compartment, or even in your wallet, so these are good areas to keep your directives handy. You will also want to include your power of attorney documents with your will, as they are legal documents.

Medical directives are a part of the foundation of any good estate plan. They give instruction to health care providers on who the decision makers are and how they will make decisions regarding the principal health care and medical treatment. These documents are vitally important if people have a religious faith that requires or disallows certain types of medical treatment.

Christopher J. Berry, Esq., Witzke Berry PLLC

Health Care Directives

Health Care Agent

I have chosen a health care agent, or durable power of attorney for health care, to manage my health care affairs should I become incapacitated. I have also named some alternatives, should that particular person not be available. They are aware of my health care wishes and are granted the authority to make certain decisions regarding my care.

Appointed Health Care Agent #1	
Appointed Health Care Agent #2	
Appointed Health Care Agent #3	
Appointed Health Care Agent #4	

Health Care Documents

I have the following documents concerning my health care wishes. The locations of those documents are listed, and they should also be found in this portfolio. Those professionals who have helped me prepare those documents are also listed.

Document	
Date Prepared	
Effective Date	
Professional's Name, Title, and Contact Information	
Location of Document	

Document	
Date Prepared	
Effective Date	
Professional's Name, Title, and Contact Information	
Location of Document	

Document	
Date Prepared	
Effective Date	
Professional's Name, Title, and Contact Information	
Location of Document	

CHAPTER 14

Durable Power of Attorney of Finances

If a person is mentally incapacitated, and no plans have been made, there is generally nothing that you can do. A guardian would have to be appointed by the court to handle your personal and financial affairs. This is usually an expensive, time consuming proposition. Prior to any incapacitation, you must take steps and arrangement for someone to handle your affairs in the event you cannot handle your affairs yourself.

Steven J. Maffei, Attorney at Law

To plan for incapacitation, a person should have a Power of Attorney, appointing a trusted individual to handle his or her financial affairs in case of incapacitation (this might also be called a Durable Power of Attorney). If a family member is incapacitated, without a Power of Attorney, the family may need to bring a court motion for conservatorship and/or guardianship. This can be a time consuming, expensive process.

Jennifer R. Lewis Kannegieter, Attorney at Law

In the last section, you dealt with a medical power of attorney. In this section, you will be dealing with a durable power of attorney over your finances. This can be the same person or someone different. You may want to consider naming a different person so there are not any conflicts of interest. This is a legal document and should be drafted by an attorney.

The person you choose for this job will have power over your finances and assets and their distribution. This durable power of attorney exists only when you are incapacitated and cannot make these decisions yourself. This person would not handle your affairs after your death. Once you are able to handle your affairs, this person will no longer be in charge.

If you do not name someone to be your durable power of attorney, your family will have to ask a judge to name someone the conservator of your estate. This can be an extensive, costly process that can be avoided by setting up a durable power of attorney and having all the arrangements made ahead of time.

There is also a non-durable power of attorney. This person can handle your affairs if you are out of the country or on a long vacation. This person can take care of your financial affairs while you are away. In the case of non-durable power of attorney, you may want to put a date on which their services will no longer be needed. If you die or become incapacitated, a non-durable power of attorney will no longer have any control, unless you have also named them your durable power of attorney.

There are a number of documents that you may need to prepare to set up a durable power of attorney. It is worth the effort if you have a number of financial matters that need to be taken care of, and you do not want to burden your family with having to go to court to seek conservatorship.

Much like a durable medical power of attorney, you may dictate exactly what they will and will not have control over. It is up to you. You should not limit their powers too much, or they will not be as effective in the role you have granted them.

In most states, you can make a durable power of attorney if you are at least 18 years of age and are of sound mind. You can grant the following powers to a durable power of attorney:

- Use your assets to pay your daily debts and expenses

- Handle your business transactions with banks and other financial institutions

- Handle real estate issues, such as buying, selling, mortgaging, and paying taxes

- File and pay your taxes

- Handle your retirement accounts

- Collect social security benefits on your behalf, as well as other governmental, military, or civic benefits

- Invest your money in stocks, bonds, and other investments

- Handle your insurance policies and buy and sell them on your behalf

- Operate your business and manage its finances

- Hire an attorney to represent you in court

- Make donations to organizations you choose

- Transfer any assets or property to a living trust

You can make any additions or restrictions to their power that you wish. They cannot do the following unless you expressly state that they can:

- Act as your medical power of attorney and make medical decisions on your behalf

- Make decisions about marriage, adoption, or voting

- Alter or create a will on your behalf

- Take over other business powers you have granted to others

You have a few options concerning when a durable power of attorney becomes effective. If you want them to take over immediately, you need to write an effective date on the documentation. Your other choice is to dictate that they can only take over if you become incapacitated and unable to take care of your financial affairs.

If you decide to allow your agent to take over some of your affairs now, this does not mean they will automatically take over everything if you become incapacitated. You need to be clear on this point, both with your agent and in your documentation.

You may at any time revoke your durable power of attorney if you choose. This will negate their control immediately, or on a date you have decided upon.

You do have a third option. You can decide to give your agent power of attorney immediately, but that they should only act when you are incapacitated. This can alleviate problems that can arise if you only appoint them upon your incapacitation, in what is referred to as a springing document.

In the situation of the springing document, a doctor must examine you and then in writing state that you are incapacitated and unable to manage your own affairs. This can be difficult, at times, and can be avoided if they are already acting as your agent. They can then make the decision to take over your affairs.

To end a durable power of attorney, there are certain circumstances that must occur.

1. **Your death:** Upon your death, a durable power of attorney no longer exists. If your agent does not know of your demise, any actions that they take on your behalf are still valid.

2. **You revoke it:** You can revoke it at any time, as long as you are of sound mind.

3. **Your agent is no longer able to serve:** If your agent no longer wants the role, or is unable to fulfill their duties, then an alternative agent will be granted the durable power of attorney, so it is important that you name one in your documents.

4. **A court of law invalidates your durable power of attorney documents:** A relative can ask a judge to appoint a conservator instead of acknowledging your durable power of attorney. It is rare, but it can happen. A judge can also make the ruling that you were not of sound mind when you created the power of attorney.

You should have a definite plan in place among your business associates and/or partners regarding to what is to be done with your share of the business once you are gone. Do you want your family members to continue to act in your place? Do the members of the business want outside interference from other family members once a person is gone (the Yoko Ono effect)? Would you want a straight liquidation so your family members can be financially taken care of out of your equity share of the business? These are all things that must be addressed immediately with the business partners. You should have an agreement in writing prepared by an attorney regarding what happens to each partner's share of the business if that person dies. I would even suggest that each member of the business get their own attorney to review the document so no conflict of interest issue could be raised at a later date.

Steven J. Maffei, Attorney at Law

You need to make sure you choose the right person to be your durable power of attorney. It should be someone who is familiar with your affairs and finances, and is dedicated to making sound decisions on your behalf.

If you have a spouse, it makes sense to consider him or her first. It not only makes legal and financial matters easier, but it also gives your spouse an emotional sense of control during a time when he or she made need and desire it. If you choose someone else, conflicts can arise over decisions made.

In certain circumstances, it may not be practical to assign your spouse as your agent. Your spouse may be elderly and ill and unable to handle this responsibility. You might want to consider a responsible child instead.

Whomever you choose, they should be someone you completely trust. If you do not trust someone enough with this kind of power, then you should not choose an agent. In this case, the court will choose and supervise someone to handle your affairs. If there is no one you trust, at least the court will be overseeing whomever they choose.

The person you choose does not have to be a business executive, but it is good idea that they have a solid head on their shoulders and are dependable and trustworthy. They can get financial assistance if they need it, but they will be making your decisions for you, not the people they are getting help from.

If you need an agent to run your business, then you may want to choose someone who is familiar with your company and has the skills to run it. An agent may also need to possess certain skills and knowledge if they are making extensive financial investments for you.

Having someone who lives close to you geographically is also a good idea. It is harder to manage your financial affairs from half way across the country. The agent may need to be on hand to pay your bills and manage your mail and other affairs that would require them to live close to you.

Sometimes families can be emotional and act in ways they would not normally when it comes to your affairs. They may be motivated by grief or greed. If you anticipate conflicts, it is a good idea to deal with them before enlisting an agent to handle your affairs. You can try to explain your wishes to those you anticipate will have problems with your decision. If you cannot reason with them, you should consult your attorney to make sure all your documents are in order so that no one can block your wishes from being carried out.

It is a good idea, in most cases, to name the same person to oversee all your affairs, both during the time you are incapacitated and upon your death. This can minimize conflicts later on between different parties. If you decide to name different people to handle different aspects of your estate, you want to make sure that they know each other and that they all get along.

Below is a list of different jobs and the title of the person who is usually assigned to do that job:

During Incapacitation	
Durable Power of Attorney for Health Care	Agent for Health Care
Durable Power of Attorney of Finances	Agent for Finances
Living Trust	Successor Trustee (This person manages property.)
After Your Death	
Will	Executor
Living Trust	Successor Trustee (In this case, they distribute property.)

One person can be assigned all these roles to minimize any problems and conflicts that may arise. In the case of your finances, you can name more than one agent. This is not advisable unless the circumstances warrant more than one person. There can be conflicts and differences of opinion, and having two agents can lock up your estate if they do not agree with one another. In these cases, the two agents could be forced to fight out their differences in court, which can further delay the settling of your estate. It might be hard to choose just one person, because others' feelings may be hurt, but you must look at it from a business and practical side rather than an emotional one.

> I generally recommend one person for the bills, but that may not be the same for other financial matters. The medical decision maker may be different as well. Some people are better with emotional decisions, while others are better with organizing and finances.
>
> Jane S Eddy, ChFC, CLU

The following forms are for a durable and non-durable power of attorney. These should be included in your portfolio and can also be found on the CD-ROM attached to this book. You can fill these forms out, and they can be revoked at anytime. If you have any concerns, you should ask your attorney.

Durable Power of Attorney for Finances

This section contains my durable power of attorney information. The document I am including is durable, which means it remains effective after I am incapacitated and unable to manage my own affairs. It should be noted that if I die, all the powers granted here will be terminated unless I have made other arrangements to grant similar powers in my will or a similar document. The information about who will then handle my affairs can be found in section #_____ which deals with my will and trust.

Document Title	
Date Prepared	
My Designated Agent's Name	
My Designated Alternate Agents' Names	
When it will be Effective	
Professional Assistance Provided	
Professional Assistance	
Name, Title, and Contact Information	
The Location of the Original Documents	
Any other Instructions	

Temporary Financial Powers of Attorney

These documents are not durable. If I become incapacitated, they will no longer be valid.

Document Title	
Date Prepared	
My Designated Agent's Name	
My Designated Alternate Agents' Names	
When it will be Effective	
Professional Assistance Provided	
Professional Assistance	
Name, Title, and Contact Information	
The Location of the Original Documents	
Any other Instructions	

Document Title	
Date Prepared	
My Designated Agent's Name	
My Designated Alternate Agents' Names	
When it will be Effective	
Professional Assistance Provided	
Professional Assistance	
Name, Title, and Contact Information	
The Location of the Original Documents	
Any other Instructions	

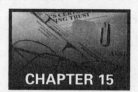

CHAPTER 15

Organ Donation

If you do not intend to be an organ donor, you may skip this section. Thinking about organ donation can make some people squeamish, but it can save or improve a life after you have passed on. There are some religions that are opposed to organ donation, and if this is the case, you might want to at least leave a note concerning this in this section of your portfolio.

When you die, or even if you are expected to not recover, your loved ones will be asked whether they want your organs donated or even about having your whole body donated for science. This is an extremely hard decision to place on loved ones who are just coming to grips with your death or incapacitation. It is far better to make a decision ahead of time, and let your loved ones know what that decision is. If you have a health care power of attorney, they need to know what your decision is.

There are close to 100,000 people in America waiting for organ transplant surgery. Each state has its own registry for organ donation. You may visit **http://www.organdonor.gov/donor/registry.shtm** for a complete list for each state. You can then designate on your driver's license whether you are an organ donor, and there will be a symbol placed on your license. You can also carry a donor card with you. You can download these from **http://organdonor.gov/donor/index.htm**.

Assuming that you wish to be a donor, when you die, a medical decision will be made as to whether your organs or tissue are able to be used for a transplant. Organs and tissues can also be used for medical research. If you wish for your whole body to be donated, it is sent to a medical school for research and instruction. There is no expense for organ donation, but sometimes, there may be fees for whole body donations. It is best to find out while you are making your decisions. Whole body donation arrangements will usually have to be made by you prior to your death. Because you will be donating your whole body, you will not have a funeral with a burial. You may have a memorial service in your honor instead.

With whole body donations, a medical school will cremate your remains and spread them on a particular plot. You can choose to have your remains returned to your family for burial or cremation, but these arrangements need to be made ahead of time, and your family can expect to wait a year or two. Choosing to donate your body does not mean that a medical school will accept it. The way in which you died, any disease you may have had, or just the fact that the school does not need a body at the time you die can all be reasons for rejection. It is recommended that you have a backup plan for burial in case of body rejection.

Typical organs and tissues that are transplanted include:

Skin	Corneas
Liver	Heart
Kidneys	Lungs
Pancreas	Connective tissues

Many tissues and organs donated are used for scientific research. Organ donation for transplants is much trickier, and only about 1 percent of donors is compatible with those who are on waiting lists for organs.

Timing is crucial in organ donation. The longer the time between death and removal, the less likely the organ or tissue is to be useable. That is why families are often pushed to make a decision quickly, or even before you die. A body must be pronounced dead and unable to be revived. There is considerable controversy about how long a period to wait, as bodies have been revived up to five minutes after the heart has stopped. This is why having a medical directive is important, as is documentation about donation. Seconds count for the viability of organs.

Once a body has been determined dead, then it is connected to a respirator to ensure blood flow to the organs. Then, the organ or organs can be removed for a transplant. This procedure can take up to 24 hours. The good news is that you can have an open-casket funeral with an organ donation. It does not disfigure the body in any way that can be seen.

Make sure that you document in your health care directives that you wish to be an organ donor. You should carry an organ donor card at all times. And most important, you need to inform those who need to make decisions what your wishes are concerning organ donation.

If you wish to find out information about whole body donation and medical schools that accept donations, you can contact the National Anatomical Service at 800-727-0700. They have listings of the medical school most in need of cadavers.

If you need more information or help with tissue or organ donation, you can go to **www.donatelife.net**, or call them at 804-782-4920.

In this section of your portfolio, include any documents concerning organ donation, including a copy of your organ donation card.

Organ Donation

Included in this section of my portfolio is information concerning the question of organ, tissue, or whole body donation. My wishes are spelled out here clearly.

_ I wish to donate _ (organ) _ (tissue) _ (whole body) after my death.

_ I do not wish for any part of my body to be donated for transplant or medical research.

(Please note that if the answer to the above question is no, then nothing more needs to be filled out in this section of the portfolio. It is recommended that this first statement be included, even if you do not want to donate your organs, so that your family knows your wishes.)

Arrangements for Donation

Contact information for the receiving organization	
Location of any additional documents	
My wishes concerning burial and alternate plans	

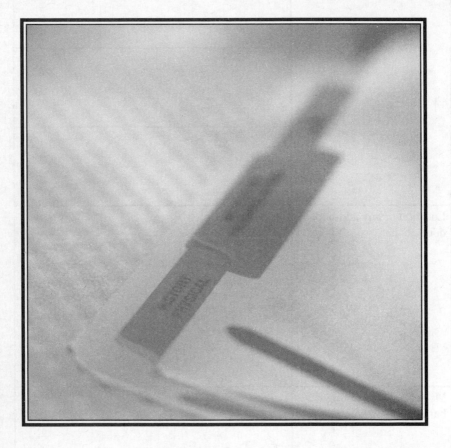

CHAPTER 16

Your Burial Arrangements

Burial arrangements can be the largest financial burden placed on your loved ones. Just as they are dealing with the emotions of your passing and questions concerning other financial matters, such as paying the mortgage or keeping the company going, they have to choose burial plots, flower arrangements, funeral homes, and caskets. The more planning and arrangements that you can do ahead of time, the better off you will leave your family. Funerals can be expensive. You can relax a little after you have made these arrangements, because you will leave your family with a solid plan, and they will not have to make these hard decisions under stress.

One of the first questions that must be answered is whether you wish to be buried or cremated. Making this decision, and following up with the arrangements, can save your family time, stress, and even cost. You can have a funeral paid off before you die, if you wish, and some funeral homes have different packages that include ceremony, casket or urn, and even the burial plot. You also have the luxury to shop around and find the best prices, rather than relying on your loved ones to make quick choices under the pressure of time.

Burial

This is the most common decision people make concerning how they want their body disposed of. Burial can take place immediately, or there can be a delay based upon religious preferences and making sure family members can travel to where you are being laid to rest. This is usually accompanied by a funeral or a memorial service.

A body can be buried underground or placed within a crypt or mausoleum. Most burials include a viewing of a body in a casket. Some cemeteries require a casket, while others may not. There are no US laws making it mandatory to have a casket for burial. The embalming process is also not mandated. A body can be refrigerated instead of embalmed and can remain so even if the burial is not scheduled for a few days.

Costs of a Burial

As I mentioned earlier, you have some options about payment for a burial if you pay ahead. You can pay the entire cost, make payments, or make plans and leave enough money for your loved ones to cover the costs. Whatever your payment plans are, place the information in this section of your portfolio.

If you decide to just leave the money for your loved ones, you have the option of setting up what is called a Totten Trust. This is an account that is payable upon death. You can set up an account, such as a bank account or money market account, and name a beneficiary. They can then withdraw the money only upon your death. The good news is that it is not subject to probate. You need to let your beneficiary know about this account so that they can access the necessary funds for your funeral arrangements.

The average cost for a funeral is about $6,500, according to the National Director's Association. This can be more or less, according to your needs.

I have included a table of costs that can be used as a reference when making a decision concerning your burial arrangements.

Embalming	$400	Body Preparation	$150
Funeral Home cost	$1500	Casket	$2000
Viewing	$300	Burial Vault	$500
Hearse (local)	$200	Plot	$700
Service car	$80	Digging	$500

Be advised that sometimes, the costs of digging and other services can double over the weekend, and after 3 p.m. on weekdays.

Cremation

The number of people choosing cremation has risen over the past few decades, and now, about 30 percent of people choose cremation. The cost is significantly less than a burial, at about $400 to $600. You have the option of burying the remains, scattering them, or placing them in an urn. The body is usually placed in a temporary casket that is made of just plain wood, cardboard, or even canvas.

You have a few options for a funeral or memorial service along with a cremation.

- Cremation with no service
- Cremation first, then memorial service or funeral
- Funeral service and viewing, then cremation
- Funeral service, cremation, then memorial service without remains present

If you choose to have a funeral or viewing of the body, you can rent a casket for this purpose. You must rent the casket from the mortuary or from a casket company. Your family cannot be charged an extra fee for renting a casket from somewhere else, nor are they required to rent or buy a casket from the mortuary.

The fees for a cremation may include viewing of the body, transportation to a crematorium, cremation, a container for the ashes, a memorial service, a death certificate, an obituary, and scattering of the remains. If you wish to have a cremation and the scattering at sea, this can raise the cost by about $2,000. If you wish for the remains to be placed in a niche at a columbarium, this will cost from $1,000 to $6,000.

You have some options of what to do with the remains from a cremation.

- Have them placed in a mausoleum or columbarium. These are located in churches, cemeteries, and even some colleges.

- Have them buried in a cemetery plot.

- Have them buried on family property (check local and state regulations).

- Keep the ashes at home.

- Have the remains divided amongst family members.

- Scatter the remains. This can be done by the funeral home, a clergy person, or a family member. Most of the time, you can scatter them over public land, waterways, or private property (check your local and state laws).

There are some other options available now for cremation ashes.

- Turning the ashes into a diamond. The carbon extracted from cremated remains and used to create a real diamond of differing sizes, colors, and cuts.

- Ashes can be suspended in blown glass.

- Ashes can be mixed into a planting soil to plant a memorial plant or flower.

There are many types of urns you can choose from as well.

- Standard urns: These are made from a variety of materials in many styles.

- Scattering urns: These are used for scattering ashes. Some of these can be kept and used as a birdhouse or saved as a memorial.

- Biodegradable urns: These can be left in nature and break down naturally in the environment.

- Cremation jewelry: This is designed to hold a little bit of the ash.

You can find more creation memorial options at **http://www. cremationsolutions.com**.

Embalming Issues

The process of embalming involves removing the blood and replacing it with a fluid that preserves the body. Good refrigeration can create the same effect, although embalming is the standard practice. There is a myth that a body must be embalmed after death. There is some truth to this, but for the most part, embalming is not necessary. The instances in which a body has to be embalmed are:

- If a body has to be transported by plane or train over state or country lines

- If there is a long period of time between death and the time the body is scheduled to be buried

- If a communicable disease was involved with the death

As long as your body is refrigerated, you do not need to be embalmed. Funeral services can proceed as normal. Instead of weeks, a body that has not been embalmed will begin to decompose in days. If you choose not to be embalmed, you can save your family around $400. The rate of refrigeration is usually less than $50 a day.

Caskets

Once you have decided between burial and cremation, there are some further issues to consider. If you are having a burial, you need to decide upon a casket, and if you have decided on cremation, you may have to decide which urn you might want. It may not be something that you want to think about or deal with, but you can save your loved ones a lot of money by doing some comparison shopping. Urns and caskets have the largest markup of any other funeral product or service.

In consideration of a casket, you must think about whether you will be buried underground and how soon you will be buried after your death. A simple pine box is really all that is needed for an immediate burial. If you plan to have a viewing, you might consider a more luxurious casket. There are many different types of caskets and materials that they are made from.

If you are going to be cremated, you may want to have a funeral or memorial service prior to your cremation. In this case, your family can just rent a casket. It does not need to be cremated along with the body. This set up is used quite often.

With a casket, you can choose different woods, linings, and you can even choose gold hinges if you like. The choice is totally up to you. The cost can run upwards of tens of thousands of dollars. You also have of the choice of where you get your casket from. A funeral home cannot force you to buy one of theirs. If you need some help finding a casket and comparing prices, here are some places you can check:

- **www.casketxpress.com**

- **www.funerals.org**

- **www.batesville.com**

- **www.casketgallery.com**

- **www.CasketSite.com**

- **www.DignifiedCaskets.com**

- **www.BestPriceCaskets.com**

Urns

If you decide that you want your ashes scattered, the funeral home can provide you with a temporary urn, or you can choose to buy a fancier one on your own. If you decide that you want your remains buried or placed in a columbarium, then an urn will need to be purchased.

Like caskets, urns can be made from many different materials, and the prices can range from relatively inexpensive, to very expensive. If you plan to have a burial at sea, a biodegradable urn works best.

Below are some resources if you are interested in buying an urn:

- **www.cremationassociation.org**

- **www.cremation.com**

- **www.cremation.org**

- **www.Urnexpress.com**

- **www.seaservices.com**

- **www.Memorial-Urns.com**

- **www.urnseller.com**

Burial Markers

If you decide that you want to be buried, the next decision you should make is what type of burial marker or headstone you wish to have. Traditional headstones are used with in-ground burials. Flat grave markers can be used with an in-ground burial, but are also attached to a burial vault above ground. These types of markers are also used with mausoleums, columbariums, and family crypts. If the particular graveyard you are being buried in has some space constraints, they may prefer that you use a burial marker, which looks much like a plaque.

Like other funeral products, the materials, sizes, and shapes of burial markers and headstones have a wide range. The price of these items has a wide range as well. Here are some costs to consider:

Bronze Marker	$3,000	Burial Plot	$280,000
Granite Marker	$1,000	Burial Permit	$10
Granite Marker upright	$10,000	Vase	$100
Marble Statue	$20,000	Individual Crypt/Mausoleum	$20,000
Crypt	$50,000	Family Crypt	$2,000,000

Some sources to research prices and what you might need include:

- www.MonumentBuilders.org

- www.BurlesonMonuments.com

- www.NorthlakeMemorial.com

- www.westmemorials.com

- www.headstones.net

- www.artisanmemorials.com

- www.monumentsinstone.com

Epitaphs and Other Extras

An epitaph is a something that is written on your marker or headstone. It can be as simple as your name and dates of birth and death. It can also contain other information, such as your status as a mother and loving wife. You can leave a saying or a prayer as part of your epitaph.

You can add things to your marker, such as your picture, sound, music, and even lights. Many stones have a built in vase to place flowers in. You can pay an extra fee to have flowers and decorations changed for the seasons on your burial site by the cemetery or memorial society.

If you are a veteran, the Department of Veterans Affairs will provide a flag for your casket or urn. You can contact them at **www.cem.va.gov** for more details.

Final Touches

It is the attention to fine details that can make the process of your burial so much easier on your family. One of those details is what you intend to wear for your funeral. You might have a favorite suit or outfit that you wish to wear. Make sure that this outfit is accessible and that you note your wishes in your portfolio. There may be certain jewelry or vestments that you wish to be adorned in. You may also wish that certain pictures are added or certain items. All of this information needs to be available for your loved ones so that they know clearly what your wishes are.

The following forms are for the disposition of your remains and contain your wishes concerning this subject. There are forms about your burial clothes, head stone, casket or urn, and epitaph. You should also fill out the form about how you intended the family to pay for all these items, and add the forms to your portfolio. You can also find a copy on the CD-ROM attached to this book.

> Most states have their laws available online, but these Web sites may not always be easy to read or up to date. If a person finds information online from a site that is not state-specific, it is a good idea to cross-reference that information with a state-specific site. Many counties also have law libraries where a person can go and read the statutes or find other information on the law.
>
> Jennifer R. Lewis Kannegieter, Attorney at Law

Disposition of Remains

This section will either contain burial instructions or cremation instructions. Here, you will find all the information you will require about my wishes concerning the disposal of my remains. Information about the actual funeral or memorial service is contained in a different section of my portfolio.

I wish for my remains to be handled in the following manner:
❏ Burial   ❏ Cremation

Burial

[ ] I prefer burial. Chose your burial preferences below.		
[ ] Immediate [ ] After Services	[ ] Embalm [ ] Do Not Embalm	[ ] In Ground [ ] Above Ground

Contact Information for those handling Burial	
Where I wish to be Buried and Contact Information	
Location of Burial Documents	

Cremation

[ ] I prefer cremation. Chose your cremation preferences below.		
Cremation [ ] Immediate [ ] After Services	**Embalming** [ ] Embalm [ ] Do Not Embalm	**Placement** [ ] Niche in Columbarium [ ] Burial [ ] Scattered [ ] To Individual

Contact Information For Those Handling Burial of Cremated Remains	
Where I Wish Cremated Remains to be Buried and Contact Information	
Location of Burial Documents	

Casket

Material	[ ] Wood Type:	[ ] Metal Type:	[ ] Other Type:
Model Number or Design			
Exterior Finish			
Interior Finish			
Cost Preference	Approx. $		
Instructions			

Urn

Material	[ ] Wood Type:	[ ] Metal Type:	[ ] Other Type:
Model Number or Design			
Exterior Finish			
Interior Finish			
Cost Preference	Approx. $		
Instructions			

Headstone, Monument, or Burial Marker

Preference	
Material	
Design Name or Model Number	
Interior Finish	
Finish	
Instructions	

Epitaph

Placement	
Inscription	
Instructions	

Extras

Item	
Inscription	
Instructions	

Item	
Inscription	
Instructions	

Burial Clothes

This section contains my preferences for clothing for burial or cremation.

Clothing, Accessory, or Other Item	Location of Items	Does Item Need to be removed before Cremation or Burial
		[ ] Yes [ ] No
		[ ] Yes [ ] No
		[ ] Yes [ ] No
		[ ] Yes [ ] No
		[ ] Yes [ ] No
		[ ] Yes [ ] No
		[ ] Yes [ ] No
Additional Instructions		

Financial Concerns

I have listed the cost of certain items and what has already been paid. All the necessary papers and receipts should be included in this section of the portfolio.

Item or Service	Cost	Balance Due
Casket		
Urn		
Cremation		
Burial service		
Burial site		
Casket rental		
Disposal fee (such as scattering of ashes)		
Special fees (such as creating a cremation diamond)		
Plaque		
Headstone		
Death Certificate fee		

I have an account that is to be used as a funeral cost account and can be accessed upon my death.

Location of the Account:
Account #:
Beneficiary on the Account:
Amount in the Account:
Money should be used for:
Documents concerning account can be located:

CHAPTER 17

Funeral Decisions

In the previous chapter, you made decisions regarding your burial and cremation wishes and plans. In this section of your portfolio, you will include information about your funeral and memorial service.

At a time when emotions are high, family members can often get into debates about funeral services. With there being a time crunch, emotions can flare. If you have stated exactly how you want services to be run, where, and by whom, you can effectively reduce the stress and provide relief to your loved ones. It is your funeral, so you should have the choice of how it should run. It will be the last gathering you will get to plan and execute.

As we begin, let me define the difference between a funeral and a memorial service. The biggest difference is that at a funeral, the body is present, and at a memorial service, it is not.

Depending on your religious beliefs and the needs of your family, there may be a number of different services and ceremonies. The funeral usually occurs just prior to the burial or cremation of the body. There are other ceremonies, such as wakes and visitations, that can occur. The length, number, and size of each of these gatherings may differ among religions, cultures, and traditions.

Viewing

A viewing occurs prior to a funeral. It is a time when people can come to see your body and pay their last respects. The body may be in a casket or laid out. This can occur in a funeral home, church community center, or even the person's home.

Visitation

A visitation is similar to a viewing. Usually, the family is present while people view the body and visit and reconnect with family and friends. They spend time reflecting and honoring your life.

Wake

A wake is a time when the family and friends get together to mourn and celebrate your life at the same time. Wakes can take days and usually involve considerable eating and drinking. Most of the time, a wake takes place in a person's home, but funeral homes and other large halls are an option.

The term "wake" refers to waking the dead in Irish traditions. There is loud wailing, talking, laughing, and crying. There are wake traditions in Japan that involve chanting, smoke, and prayers. There are many different versions of the wake in different cultures, and each has its set of rules and traditions.

If you choose to have a wake, visitation, or viewing, here are some items you may wish to consider:

- Where it will be located

- When it will occur

- What should occur at the event

- Who will be invited

- Who will be in charge

- What casket will be used and whether it will need to be rented

- What food, drink, music, speeches, or other events will occur

- Any special requests of what should occur at particular events

Memorial Service

Since the body does not need to be present for a memorial service, the details can be more flexible. Some services do not occur until months or years after a death. Sometimes, it is not practical to have a service right away that will include all your family and friends. You may want a small funeral and then a memorial service later on to give people time to make travel plans. Having the memorial service days after allows more people to come and allows the body to be buried or cremated within a few days without rushing people to attend. Sometimes, the anniversary of a death is a good time to have a memorial service.

Memorial services can take place anywhere, since there is not a body involved. These types of services are usually not expensive and allow for more people to attend. You should make your thoughts on having a memorial service clear. There may be those who oppose this type of service in contrast to a full funeral service. If you wish to save your family some money, then a memorial service is the better solution. You can decide who will attend, what will be said, and where it will be located. Family members are more likely to follow your instructions to have a memorial service if they are clearly written out in your portfolio.

Funerals

These are services in which the body is often present, and they occur prior to burial or cremation. These ceremonies are generally short and often take place in the funeral home or church. It is a religious sending of the soul. Funerals can have an open or closed casket, per your request.

Sometimes, a funeral will be accompanied by a mass, or other religious ceremony, depending on your particular religion or culture. Military personnel can request to have a military funeral. At these types of funerals, Taps is played, a flag is presented, and sometimes, a gun salute is included. If you need more information about a military funeral, go to **www.militaryfuneralhonors.osd.mil**.

In some cases, only family and close invited friends will attend a funeral, while the general public and other friends will attend other events and ceremonies. This decision should be made with your family. In some situations, the funeral is the largest public event.

Following are some items you may wish to consider as you are planning your funeral.

- Where the funeral will take place

- When the funeral will take place

- Who will attend the funeral

- Who will preside over the ceremony

- What music should be played

- What type of eulogy you want

- Whether you want specific people to speak at your funeral

- Whether you want an open or closed casket

- How you want the casket or urn displayed

- Whether you want people to send flowers or donate to a memorial or charity

Who will Preside?

Selecting who will preside over your funeral is an important decision. Often, people will choose their spiritual leader. You may choose a close friend or a member of a fraternal organization you belong to. If you choose a close friend or family member, they may be emotional and have a hard time leading a funeral service. Take your time, and consider your decision carefully. Once you choose who will preside over your funeral, you should speak with them and talk about what your wishes are concerning it.

Casket and Urn Issues

In the last chapter, you learned about the options for selecting the right urn or casket. If something happened that disfigured your body, you of course would have a closed casket. You have other decisions to make, such as whether words are going to be said over the casket graveside, or whether the casket will be lowered at the conclusion of the funeral service.

You may have chosen to rent a casket for the funeral service, in which case your body will need to be transferred to another casket, or prepared for cremation. Many of these details will be worked out with a funeral director, but if you have any special instructions, you need to include them in your portfolio.

Included in your decisions about your casket are pallbearers. These are the people who carry the casket to and from the place where a funeral is held. They also carry the casket from the vehicle to the burial site. If you wish to have pallbearers, make sure that you name them in your portfolio. Usually, the number of pallbearers ranges from four to eight people, but try to keep the number even so that there is a balanced number on each side of the casket. It might be a good idea to name a few extra pallbearers in case the original ones cannot serve in that capacity.

You should also choose how your casket will arrive at the graveside. Most mortuaries have their own vehicles to transport caskets. You can choose a different vehicle, or even pick a horse drawn carriage if you prefer. You may choose the type of vehicle that you want used, but you should check with the policies of the funeral home. Some funeral homes will charge you a transportation fee, even if you supply your own vehicle. You should plan ahead, decide what is important to you regarding transportation, and make the necessary arrangements.

Even if you have a full funeral service elsewhere, you may also decide that you want a small service graveside. This usually involves someone saying a few words before the casket is buried. You can decide who should be there and what it is you want said. Be sure to include all these plans in your portfolio, and, if possible, you should let those involved know what your plans are ahead of time.

After the Funeral

After the memorial service or funeral, you may want to plan a reception. This allows your family and friends to get together for support and to reflect and celebrate your life. A reception can be similar to a wake in that it usually involves eating, drinking, and sometimes celebration. These types of receptions can be held in the home or in a larger place, like a church hall or community center. You should make some decisions ahead of time concerning the reception.

- Who will attend

- Where it will be held

- What food and drink will be included

- What music will be played

- Whether there will be other activities or entertainment

There a few final points to consider when planning a funeral that shouldn't be overlooked:

- Who will be in charge of contacting friends and family to let them know about your funeral or memorial service

- Where the money will come from to pay for the funeral services

- A list of who should be invited to the funeral or memorial service

- What arrangements need to be made for friends and relatives coming from out of town

- Who will be in charge of food and drink

- Who will be in charge of making any final arrangements

- Where will people call to find out about final arrangements

- Whether there will be a Web site with information about funeral or memorial services

Make sure this section of your portfolio includes any plans, receipts, and information about your services and ceremonies. If you have any contracts, outstanding bills, or any other related information, they should be included, or a reference given to where these documents can be located. Below are forms you should fill out and place in your portfolio. They include all your wishes concerning your funeral or memorial service.

Funeral Arrangements

This section will include information about my funeral, memorial service, or any other gathering and ceremony associated with my death. Any information regarding my casket, urn, or burial instructions can be found in section # of this portfolio.

Viewing, Visitation, or Wake

Type of Gathering	
Location of Gathering and Venue Information	
Preplanned Arrangements	

Body Present [ ] Yes [ ] No	Body Present [ ] Yes [ ] No	Casket Included [ ] Yes [ ] No
Invitations to gathering will be [ ] Public [ ] Private	When the gathering should occur	
Instructions		

Type of Gathering	
Location of Gathering and Venue Information	
Preplanned Arrangements	

Body Present [ ] Yes [ ] No	Body Present [ ] Yes [ ] No	Casket Included [ ] Yes [ ] No
Invitations to gathering will be [ ] Public [ ] Private	When the gathering should occur	
Instructions		

Type of Gathering	
Location of Gathering and Venue Information	
Preplanned Arrangements	

Body Present [ ] Yes [ ] No	Body Present [ ] Yes [ ] No	Casket Included [ ] Yes [ ] No
Invitations to gathering will be [ ] Public [ ] Private	When the gathering should occur	
Instructions		

The next section will have instructions on whether I want a funeral and/or a memorial service.

Memorial Service

Location of Service and Contact Information	
Preplanned Arrangements	

Other Items to include at service [ ] Photo — Location: _____ [ ] Other: _____

Flower Request	Who should be invited	When service should occur

Funeral

Location of Service and Contact Information	
Preplanned Arrangements	

Body or Urn Present [ ] Yes [ ] No	The Casket shall be [ ] Yes [ ] No	Other Items to include in casket or with urn are [ ] Photo — Location: _____ [ ] Other: _____
Flower Request	Who should be invited	When service should occur

Type of Funeral Service	Person presiding over service	Person facilitating funeral arrangements
	Name	Name
	Contact Information	Contact Information

Persons doing a Eulogy		
Name	Name	Name
Contact Information	Contact Information	Contact Information

What Music Should be played and by whom

What Readings shall be included and who will read them

Pallbearers		
Name	Name	Name
Contact Information	Contact Information	Contact Information

Name	Name	Name
Contact Information	Contact Information	Contact Information

Name	Name	Name — Alternate
Contact Information	Contact Information	Contact Information

Name	Name	Name — Alternate
Contact Information	Contact Information	Contact Information

Graveside Service Instructions	How Body will be Transported

Reception Following Service

Location of Reception and Contact Information	
Preplanned Arrangements	
Who Should be Invited	
Music, Entertainment, and Activities	
Food and Drink to be Served	

Financial Concerns

I have listed the cost of funeral-related services and goods and what has already been paid. All the necessary papers and receipts should be included in this section of the portfolio.

Service	Cost	Balance Due
Memorial Service		
Funeral		
Wake		
Visitation		
Viewing		
Clergy		
Flowers		
Food and Drink		
Transportation		
Music/Entertainment		
Travel/Lodging		

I have an account that is to be used as a funeral cost account and can be accessed upon my death.

Location of the Account:
Account #:
Beneficiary on the Account:
Amount in the Account:
Money should be used for:
Documents concerning account can be located:

CHAPTER 18

Last Words

> When my obituary notice at last appears in The Times, and they say: "What, I thought he died years ago," my ghost will gently chuckle.
>
> Somerset Maugham

Sometimes, what you say after death can be more important than what you said while you were alive. An obituary is a small autobiography and retelling of your life. You want to make sure you have all the highlights included, and remove any of the low points not worth mentioning.

Writing your own obituary can be a very powerful tool. It can be a reflection upon your life that includes both joys and regrets. It can be life changing if you find that there are things you wish to accomplish before you die.

Obituaries are printed in newspapers and other publications and are a general announcement of your death. They are a small autobiography that lets other know about your life, your family, and your accomplishments. All of this is usually squeezed into a paragraph or two.

Your obituary may also contain survivors' information and information about funeral and memorial services. It may also contain information about where you wish to have donations in lieu of flowers made. This section of your portfolio will contain necessary information that helps your loved ones create an obituary that you would want.

You can approach this section in one of two ways. You may decide to write your obituary ahead of time. Upon your death, your loved ones can check it and add important information for publishing.

Your other option is to include all the information you feel could be included in your obituary and allow your loved ones to construct it. By including important biographical information in this section, you will help your loved ones create an accurate, loving obituary.

Whichever way you choose to handle your obituary, you should take time to think about what you want contained in your last words and biography for the world. In this section, you should also include where you want your obituary sent for publication.

The length of your obituary will depend upon where it is being published. It can be brief, medium-sized, or a full-length article. You can have one example of each for your loved ones to choose from so that they can send the appropriately sized one to a particular publication. If you are intending to write all three, then you should probably start with the largest, and then you can work down from there.

There is some material that you should consider including in your obituary:

- Date and place of birth

- Spouse's information

- Children's information

- Grandchildren's information

- Education information

- Employment information

- Military experience

- Significant achievements and awards

- Memberships in organizations

- Information about where to send flowers or donations

- Important information about your life

- Where you have lived

- Hobbies

You can look at newspapers and other periodicals to get an idea of what obituaries look like and what they contain. There may be a number of different places you will want your obituary sent to:

- Local newspaper

- Local newspapers of the different places you have lived and worked

- Your company newsletter

- Newsletters or other periodicals of organizations you belonged to

- Schools alumni associations and newsletters

- Magazines that may be interested in your life story

The form below should be filled out and placed in your portfolio under the obituary section. You can also find the forms on the CD-ROM that is attached to this book.

Obituary

In this section of my portfolio, you will find information concerning my obituary. I will either place a sample of the obituaries I want released or you will find the information to create your own. I have also listed the places I want my obituary sent to.

I have already drafted an obituary.   [ ]

I have left the materials for someone else to write my obituary. [ ]

Overview

Obituary Length	[ ] Small	[ ] Medium	[ ] Article Length
Include Photograph	[ ] Yes (Location: _____)		[ ] No
Publications I wish my obituary to be published in and their contact information			

Biography

Please refer to section # in this portfolio for my biographical information and information concerning my family. In addition, you may want to include the following information in my obituary.

Awards and Achievements	
Interests and Hobbies	
Personal Values and Beliefs	
Flowers Instructions	Location to send to:
Donations or Remembrances	
Other Instructions	

CHAPTER 19

Will and Trust Information

> A will contains information designating who shall be the executor of your estate, who shall be guardians of your minor children, disposition of personal property, disposition of real property, and any last wishes for the family.
>
> Gabriel Cheong, Esq., Infinity Law Group LLC

The purpose of a will is to ensure that your property is handed to those you wish. It is a legal document that should detail who will receive different assets of your estate. Much of what is contained in your portfolio will be mimicked in your will. Your portfolio is the tool that can be used to carry out the wishes described in your will. By completing your portfolio, you will have covered most of the areas that need to be dealt with in your last will and testament.

All property and assets you own at the time of your death are referred to as your estate. The process of estate planning is preparing your property and assets to be dispersed after your death. There are some other parts of estate planning, such as who will care for your young children after you are gone. Planning ahead can help in that your survivors will not be stuck in probate proceedings after you die. Probate proceedings are when the courts determine how your estate will be divided. A solid, well-written will can help avoid such proceedings.

The solution is simple: "proper planning." Proper planning will allow you to give what you have to whom you want, when you want, and in the way you want, and at the same time, allow you to pay the least amount of court costs, attorney fees, and estate taxes possible.

Mike Kilbourn, Kilbourn Associates

Probate is the court process that transfers "probate" assets upon the death of the owner. An asset is a "non-probate" asset if it is owned jointly with another person, owned by a trust, or has a designated payable-on-death or transfer-on-death beneficiary. Sometimes, avoiding probate can be as simple as making sure assets are owned, either jointly or by designating a beneficiary. Living trusts are a popular tool for avoiding probate, but unfortunately, sometimes this avenue fails because assets are not properly titled or do not get transferred to the trust.

Probate is a public proceeding, and sometimes, there are valid concerns for avoiding probate to protect privacy or avoid conflict. Before a person goes overboard trying to avoid probate, I would suggest checking into your state's probate laws and consulting with an attorney to determine whether it is advisable for the situation.

If you are planning to avoid probate, take extra care to make sure you have done everything necessary to transfer title correctly. Review your assets on a regular basis. Don't let anything slip through the cracks.

Jennifer R. Lewis Kannegieter, Attorney at Law

Most states have "Probate Code," and the local law library should have a copy available for review. There are many great resources on the Internet. Findlaw.com is a very useful resource for the pure law. Many attorneys have written articles, which are also available on the Internet, that translate the "pure law" into an understandable format for the average Joe.

David T. Pisarra, Esq.

Wills

A will is a document that you leave behind with instructions about what is to be done with your property. You are able to name people, called beneficiaries, who will receive your property. In the will, you can specify the exact property you want your beneficiaries to receive. The receiving of this property is called an inheritance.

In your will, you will also name an executor, which is the person who will take care of your affairs after you die. It is your executor who should have a copy of your portfolio. Finally, if you have minor children, you can name a guardian for them in the will, as this is the only proper place to name a guardian.

If you do not have a will at the time of your death, your estate will be intestate, which means that the state courts will determine what happens with your estate and who will be the guardian of your minor children. If you can imagine some stranger making these very important decisions, which may not coincide with your wishes, then you can realize the importance of writing a will. The court can also appoint a property guardian who will be responsible for managing your property until it can be worked out in court. It is so much easier and more practical to appoint someone yourself to take care of your children's inheritance until they reach an age where they can manage it themselves.

Any property mentioned in a will must go through probate court. This can be a long, sometimes frustrating process for your loved ones. Later in this chapter, I will mention some ways to avoid your property being locked up in probate court proceedings.

In order for someone to make a will, they must be an adult who is deemed to have a sound mind, and that must be stated in their will. In addition, for it to be legal, you must sign and date the will. When you sign it, there must be two to three witnesses. These witnesses must actually witness you signing the document. They do not need to read the will, but they must witness the signing first hand. In most states, the witnesses cannot be beneficiaries in the will.

You do not have to have your will notarized, but it is a good idea that you and the witnesses sign a sworn affidavit before a notary concerning the will. This can help in probate proceedings later on to validate the authenticity of the will. This process is called self-proving.

Unlike many other legal documents, a will does not have to be filed or recorded anywhere. You just want to make sure that it is in a safe place and that your loved ones have access to it after you die. If you do not tell anyone else where your will is, or that it even exists, you must make sure that the executor of your estate knows. You should also let them know where your portfolio is. Having the two stored together is the best idea.

When deciding to split up property, there are some things you need to be aware of. You can easily divide money among your heirs. Other types of property cannot be easily split up. It is this type of undividable property that family arguments begin over. You can try to be as fair and reasonable as possible. The more detailed your will is about certain valuable items in the estate, the less room for arguments. You should state who gets what items. You need to think about cars, jewelry, musical instruments, heirlooms, and any other item that you might have a sentimental connection to.

If there is property or a large item that you intend to leave to more than one beneficiary, it is a good idea to state what share of the item each heir will have. Sometimes, their shares may be equal, or you may decide to give a larger share to a particular heir.

You may feel compelled to dictate how your property should be handled.

You may want particular items to stay in the family or not be sold. While you can let your preferences be known, it is not always enforceable. You may want to include in your portfolio letters to your heirs expressing your wishes instead of trying to include them in your will.

> To prepare for incapacity, a person should have appointed financial and health care powers of attorney. Also, a living trust, if properly drafted, can provide instruction for incapacity through the powers of the appointed trustee.
>
> Christopher J. Berry, Esq., Witzke Berry PLLC

There are certain kinds of property that cannot be left in a will, and those exceptions are listed below:

- If someone else holds interest in a particular piece of property with you, this is referred to as a tenancy by the entirety, or a community property with a right of survivorship. In this case, the co-owner of the property will inherit your share of the property, unless they die at the same time you do.

- If you have transferred property to a living trust, you cannot then attempt to transfer it in a will.

- If you have named a beneficiary in a life insurance policy, then you cannot leave the proceeds to someone else in your will. There is no need to name the same beneficiary in your will, as this is redundant.

- As with a life insurance policy, you will name beneficiaries on your 401(k) plans, pensions, and Individualized Retirement Accounts. These beneficiaries will be named in separate documents and do not need to be named in a will, nor can you name a different beneficiary in your will.

- If you have filled out a transfer-on-death form (TOD) for your stocks and bonds, then you cannot name someone else to receive these funds in your will. You can change the name of the beneficiary on the TOD form if you wish.

- If you have a payable upon death bank account, you will have named a beneficiary. You cannot name a different recipient in your will. You can change the name on the account if you wish.

- You may have a TOD form on your vehicle. As with stocks and bonds, you cannot name someone else to inherit your car if you have filled out this form.

If you have any of the documents listed above, include them in this section of your portfolio or another appropriate section.

List as many assets as possible in TOD or POD. Keep beneficiaries on retirement plans and life insurance current. Especially for a single person, at times, it may be wise to leave some assets such as a residence in your name only, even though it will transfer through probate. Sharing ownership with a child or other may open that asset up to the other person's creditors.

Jane S Eddy, ChFC, CLU

Basically, state what you want to happen to your assets and who is responsible for making that happen. State laws govern a decedent's estate. They may require certain actions on the part of your executor, but you may have the opportunity to waive some of these actions. For example, state law may require the executor to buy a performance bond and make an accounting to the probate court. The testator (writer of the will) may be able to waive these requirements, making it easier to fulfill your wishes.

David M. Williams, CFP®

As you are creating your portfolio and creating your will, your needs and the needs of your survivors will depend on your health, wealth, resources, property, and how you live your life. You can consider the different life situations that I have illustrated below. Your particular life situation may not fit exactly into the examples, but you will get a sense of what each scenario has to offer as far as wisdom in creating your particular will.

20-Something with No Children

First, I would like to commend your foresight if you fall into this category. You may not have many assets, but you are thinking ahead. You will not have too much in the form of estate planning, but you can begin to get into the habit of developing a portfolio. If you are in the habit of it, it will grow as your assets and property grow, and you will be prepared no matter what stage of life you find yourself in.

While accidents do happen, you will not have to worry about a lengthy will and estate planning. If you have a life-threatening illness, you might find you are in a different situation. Even young people have belongings that are dear to them and that they want to pass on to certain people. Even a simple will can ensure that happens.

You may also be a self-made millionaire or have a large inheritance. If this is the case, then having a well-thought-out will is a good idea. No matter how young or healthy you are, you should at least have your health care directives in order.

Have a Partner but are not Married

In this situation, you may be living with someone but are not legally married. In some states, if you are living with someone for a certain period of time, you may be "common law" married. You need to check in your state about whether they recognize common law marriages. A common law marriage is essentially a legally recognized marriage without the benefit of a formal ceremony or registration.

If you are not married, then all your possessions will be given to your closest relatives. That is why it is so important that you make a will and complete all the necessary estate documents, to ensure your possessions are going to the people you wish for them to go to.

Have Minor Children

In this case, you need to make solid plans for your children. You must create a will in order to name a guardian for your children, as there is no other document that you can use for this purpose. You should include this information in this section of your portfolio, but you must make sure that it is clearly stated in your will.

You should consider naming a guardian in case both you and your children's other parent die or become incapacitated. Without naming someone, the court will have to appoint someone they determine fit or proper for the job. You can even create a living trust or use a will to name someone to handle the proceeds from the will designated for your children until they are old enough to manage their own finances.

Financially Stable and Midlife

In this situation, you might want to think harder about your estate and how you wish for it to be divided. If you are in good health, you still have plenty of time, but you have enough assets that it is important to have a will if an accident happens tomorrow.

If you have the means, and you don't want your family to have to be hassled with probate court, you may want to consider creating a revocable living trust. You can change this at any time while you are alive. If you die, the person you have named in the trust will then divide the proceeds of your estate without having to deal with probate. Your family will be relieved, and they can have access to necessary funds much quicker.

If you are married, there is another type of trust you can consider called an AB Trust. This type of trust avoids probate and reduces the amount of estate taxes that will have to be paid. Even if you have developed a living trust, you will still want to have a will. In case of any problems or any property not included in the living trust, a will will take care of the rest of the details of your estate. Besides, a living trust does not allow you to name a guardian for a minor child; you can only do that in a will.

Old Age or Bad Health

If you are in this situation, you need to be completing your will, and hopefully your portfolio, as quickly as possible. You can create a living trust, as mentioned in the previous section. This will help avoid probate court proceedings and potentially save in estate taxes. You should write your will immediately, or at least make sure your current will is up to date.

You should think carefully about your health, make the appropriate plans concerning your health care directives, and consider appointing a health care power of attorney. You should also consider a durable power of attorney for your finances. If you become incapacitated, they can make sure your day-to-day finances are taken care of. You can learn about power of attorney in the chapter with that heading.

Ethical, Holographic, and Oral Wills

An ethical will is not a legal will at all. It is a statement about beliefs, thoughts, and values. Earlier in the book, you were instructed how to write a letter to your loved ones, and that is an example of an ethical will. There is no property or any other inheritance associated with an ethical will.

A holographic will is one that is handwritten and not witnessed. This is legal in about half of the states; however, they are often scrutinized in probate court. There has to be a decision of whether the handwriting and signature is yours. It is much more efficient and easier to have a typed, witnessed will.

An oral will is spoken. This is the least secure type of will, as a witness must hear you dictate your last requests. This might work on a battlefield, but it is still much smarter to write a will and have it witnessed. An oral will, sometimes called a nuncupative will, is only valid in select states and is the kind most questioned and thrown out.

> You can have a will without a trust, but you cannot have a trust without a will.
>
> Gabriel Cheong, Esq. Infinity Law Group LLC

Trusts

> We tend to use revocable living trusts and other types of trusts mostly with our clients, so the will is really just there to catch anything not covered by these documents and to dispose of personal property according to the client's wishes.
>
> James F. Seramba, Grey Oak Wealth Management

Trusts are agreements that a particular person designated, a trustee, holds the legal title for property for those who are the named beneficiaries. The advantage of placing property in a trust rather than just handling it through a will is that the property is able to bypass the probate proceedings after your death.

The most basic form of a trust is a living trust. The simplest of these is an individual living trust, but if you are married, you might consider a shared living trust. To create a living trust, you must create a document called a declaration of trust. This document is similar to a will. In this declaration, you name yourself as the trustee. You can transfer some or all of your property to yourself as the trustee.

Transferring property to yourself as a trustee does not make you give up any control over that property. In the case of a shared trust, you can name both you and your spouse as co-trustees. Once you have named the trustees, you will then name the beneficiaries to take over the trust. These are the people you want to inherit the property after you are gone. This type of trust is also referred to as a revocable living trust. This means you can revoke the trust or change your beneficiaries at any time.

Once you die, the property is then turned over to the beneficiaries of the trust, also called successor trustees. They then have ownership over the property. The good news is that the transfer of property is relatively easy, and it avoids any probate hearings concerning the property.

> A good way to avoid probate court is a properly funded revocable living trust.
>
> Mike Kilbourn, Kilbourn Associates

Creating a living trust is not always the answer to transferring property. There are some circumstances you may want to consider first.

- Whether you are young and have good health. If so, then it may be better to just have a will. The exception is if you own property or have children. You can consider a living trust later in life when you have more property.

- Whether there is a better way to protect your property from having to go through probate. Later in this chapter, I will reveal some ways in which to avoid probate courts, so you might want to consider them before you consider a living trust.

- Whether there is someone you trust enough to take over ownership of the property you are considering to place in a trust. If not, then you probably should consider some other option.

- Whether you own much property. If not, then the creation of a living trust may not be worth the time and effort. In this case, probate will not be much of a hassle, so you can just create a will with all your property listed instead.

AB trusts, already discussed briefly, can save tax money for estates that are larger in size. Federal tax money is due on estates that are more substantial. The size of the estate I am referring to is one worth $2,000,000 or more. In the case of a large estate, federal taxes are owed. I will deal with taxes more in a later chapter, but for now, you should consider an AB trust because it can lower this tax burden significantly. Once the second spouse dies, a large amount of estate tax may be due.

In an AB trust, the property is protected from probate. In addition, it allows a couple to pass on property and allows the surviving spouse to live comfortably. In an AB trust, both spouses place their property into the trust. When one person dies, the other owns the property like they would in a regular living trust. Because they did not own the property outright, there will not be estate taxes owed by the survivor's estate when they pass.

In an AB trust, the couple will name final beneficiaries. These are the people who will inherit the entire estate when the last spouse dies. For example, suppose that a couple's estate is worth $2,000,000. The entire estate could be liable for estate taxes. Now suppose this couple puts in $1,000,000 each in an AB trust. Now when the first person dies, they leave $1,000,000 behind, which will not be subject to estate tax. The surviving spouse does not actually own that $1,000,000. So when the final spouse dies, her estate in the trust is only $1,000,000, and the other $1,000,000 that her husband left is also passed. Between them, they would be worth $2,000,000, and therefore, subject to estate taxes, but since each part was worth less than that, the person inheriting the two parts does not have to pay the estate taxes, because essentially, they are receiving two $1,000,000 inheritances rather than one $2,000,000 inheritance.

There are some problems with AB trusts that should be considered:

- The surviving spouse may be limited in what they can do with their spouse's property, since they do not own it outright.

- Once one of the spouses dies, the survivor must work with a lawyer and accountant to figure out how to split the estate in the trust into an irrevocable trust left by the spouse and the living trust that the surviving spouse has in their half of the trust. This can be difficult and expensive.

- The surviving spouse must submit a yearly income tax return on the irrevocable living trust of their spouse, which can be tricky for the surviving spouse to deal with annually.

- The surviving spouse must deal with record keeping. They must clearly separate their property from the property in the irrevocable trust.

- Tax laws can change, and you might owe money in the next few years that the current tax laws do not say you owe. You must be aware of these changes in tax laws, or you could end up with a large tax burden that could be eliminated in a different kind of trust.

If you are under retirement age, and your spouse dies unexpectedly, you may not want an AB trust because it will lock up your access to necessary assets and funds. You should talk to a professional estate preparer before creating this type of trust.

A simple living trust is recommended for younger people because most do not have millions of dollars in property, and they are more likely to need access to any funds left behind by their spouse. Younger people will more likely use up those assets, especially if their spouse dies unexpectedly at a young age. They can use the money or disperse it easier without worry about estate taxes, because they have time to manage it better.

Other Types of Trusts

There are other types of trusts that you can use, but they are much more complicated and do not fall within the scope of this book, which is based upon preparing your estate on your own. Most of these types of trusts are for those who are very wealthy or have unusual circumstances.

There are irrevocable trusts, such as QTIP trusts, generation skipping trusts, or charitable remainder trusts. There are special trusts that can be set up for those who are either irresponsible or handicapped in some way and cannot manage their own finances. These are referred to as spend thrift and special needs trusts.

There are also prenuptial or premarital agreements. These are created to protect property rights should someone die or decide to get divorced. In most states, your spouse is entitled to half or a third of your property when you die. This right can be waived in a marital agreement and property can be dispersed the way you want to, and this agreement trumps anything written in a will.

If you have such an agreement, then include it in your portfolio and mention it in your will. It can definitely affect how people receive their inheritance.

Even if you decide to place all your property into a trust, you still will need a will. If something happens with the trust, your will is your backup plan. If you acquire property before you die, but fail to include it in your trust, your will can take care of that property in probate. You can include a section in your will indicating that any property not included in your trust will go to a particular person. If you do not have a will, or it does not mention the property, the courts will award it to your closest relative, which may not be what you want. It is better that you are in charge of decision making rather than relying on the court system.

Executor

When you are creating your will, it is important that you choose the right person to manage your affairs. This is also true if you have a trust and have named a successor trustee. It is a good idea to also choose an alternate person in case the person you have chosen cannot perform their duty. It is your executor or your successor trustee that you are creating your portfolio for.

Here are some things to consider when choosing an executor or successor trustee:

- When choosing a person, you must keep in mind that there

may be considerable work and responsibilities involved. You may be inclined to choose your spouse or someone else close to you, but they may be grieving, and the responsibility of being the executor may be too much to handle. The process of settling your estate can take months or years.

- They must be a strong person who can deal with beneficiaries and relatives who may challenge your will and your wishes. They must be committed to executing your will and handling your estate the way you have instructed.

- They must have the ability to be assertive when necessary. They most also have a high level of integrity and honesty.

- They should be an organized person and able to handle tricky financial situations that may arise. They will have to be a master of all trades at times, and have the endurance to see the settlement of your estate, even if it takes a while.

- They must possess good, clear communication skills. They will have to work with attorneys, tax experts, accounts, and every manner of professional. They will also have to communicate clearly and honestly with your heirs as they are seeking answers.

- They should get along well with others. They must have conflict resolution skills and be able to act under pressure and duress.

- Your executor must have the time and resources to handle the tasks that need to be completed on your estate. They must be able to dedicate the time necessary to get the job done right.

In an earlier chapter, I discussed a power of attorney agent. They must possess many of the same skills and are bound by similar restrictions. It is better to pick someone who lives close or has a place to stay, because they have business concerning your estate in which they need to be present for long periods of time. There are even some states that restrict the use of nonresident executors. You should check with your state laws before trying to use a nonresident executor.

You do have the choice of naming an institution as your executor, rather than a person, although this is not recommended. There are certain situations in which a professional institution may be preferable, such as having a large or very complex estate. You will definitely want to discuss with the particular institution your desire for them to be your executor. Many institutions will not want to take on the job; some will if they know what your particular situation is and have worked with you for some time. If your estate is rather large, this is more of an enticement for an institution to take over because their entitlement to money will be more substantial.

Similar to the case of picking a financial agent, you can choose to have more than one executor. However, if you choose more than one person to handle your estate, they are more likely to have disagreements and arguments about how things should be handled. If they are disagreeing, they can hold up the estate.

Even if you have a will and a trust, you should use the same person as your executor and your successor trustee. If you are compelled to name more than one person, you should be assured that they get along and work well together. Your decision should not be based upon hurting someone's feelings by not picking them to be your executor; rather, you should make a decision based upon the best person for the job and the easiest, most efficient way to manage your estate.

You should name an alternate, as there are a number of different circumstances that could arise in which the primary people you have chosen cannot do the job. The people you assign as alternates will be used in the order your chose them. You should refer back to the characteristics you used in choosing a primary executor when choosing an alternate. This is not a popularity contest, or about who is loved the best. This is a business decision made by choosing the best person for the job.

Keeping in mind that you are performing a business transaction, you must realize you will be compensating the executor for their time. An executor is entitled to a certain amount of compensation for performing their duty. You can set a certain amount in your will, and it can be based upon what your particular state law allows.

Most executors should not expect compensation unless your estate is particularly difficult to manage or takes a while to settle. The reason is, they will more than likely be receiving an inheritance themselves. If an executor is paid a fee for their work, the compensation is taxable. They are better off accepting an inheritance, which is not taxable. If it is the case that the person is not receiving any inheritance, then you should specify a certain fee that they can expect for their services. Once you have chosen a particular person to be your executor or successor trustee, you should make them familiar with your will and your portfolio and try to answer any questions that they may have.

> You can find most information regarding the state laws on a Web site. If that is a problem, then call the local clerk of court's estate division and ask them where you can access a copy of the rules on estates. Often, the local clerk of court's estates division will have a handout on the estate rules.
>
> Stephen L. Smith, Esq., Horack, Talley, Pharr & Lowndes, P.A.

Probate

Whenever you leave a will in which property needs to be distributed, it must be filed in court through a process called probate. It is during this process that assets are gathered, documents are located and filed, and debts and taxes are paid. It is only after all these monies are taken care of that a court will begin the process of releasing the estate to be dispersed, as requested in the will, with whatever funds are left.

Probate is a long process that has drawbacks. It can tie up an estate for months, or even years, while debts and taxes are paid. Probate is expensive because attorney's fees and court costs can eat up around 5 percent of the estate. You can avoid much of the hassle of probate by following some of the tips I have outlined for you.

Probate Avoidance Techniques

Avoidance Technique	How It is Accomplished
Knowing state laws about probate proceedings	You need to check with your particular state's laws. You may qualify for proceedings designed for small estates. This process makes it easier for your inheritors to get their property. Sometimes, all it takes is an affidavit. There are procedures in place to help speed the estate through the process.
	If you are allowed to submit affidavits, then there is no need for a court hearing. This is allowed if your estate is under a certain size. If this is the case, the person who is set to inherit property from the estate needs to prepare a short document that states that they are entitled to the property mentioned in the will. They then swear to the paper under oath, and it becomes an affidavit. Once a financial institution receives the affidavit and death certificate, they can then release the funds or property.
	The other option for small estates is a minimized version of probate court. This is available in some states. In these small probate procedures, it is usually small enough that a lawyer is not needed for the proceedings.

Avoidance Technique	How It is Accomplished
Revocable Living Trust	You can transfer your property to a living trust, and it bypasses the probate process.
Making gifts while you are alive	Why wait to give your loved ones what you want to when you are dead? You can give property away as a gift. You will lose control over that property, and it will reduce the amount of property that will have to be dealt with in probate. You need to check the laws, because large gifts can be taxable. You are limited to giving $12,000 a year before the money is subject to federal gift tax. If you are able to give away enough of your assets, your estate may be eligible for the small probate proceedings.
Designating a Beneficiary	You can designate a beneficiary on bank accounts, pensions, retirement accounts, and some securities. You may need to check your states laws, as some do not allow beneficiaries on securities. When you create accounts, such as a 401(k), you will be given a page to fill out to name a beneficiary. The funds will go to that beneficiary without having to go through probate.
Vehicle Beneficiary	In some states, you can list a beneficiary for your car, and therefore, it would not need to be dealt with in probate. You can check with your department of motor vehicles if you live in Ohio, Missouri, Kansas, Connecticut, or California, as these are the only states that have these kinds of laws.
TOD for Real Estate	There are some states that allow real estate to be transferred to a beneficiary upon death, and therefore, not be subject to probate court. You can check with the office of deeds in Ohio, Nevada, New Mexico, Missouri, Kansas, Colorado, Arkansas, or Arizona, as these are the only states currently with these kinds of laws. In order to benefit from a TOD, you must fill out a transfer-on-death deed. This must be signed and notarized, and then it has to be filed in the county land records office. The deed will state that it will not take effect until your death. You can choose to revoke the deed anytime before your death.

Avoidance Technique	How It is Accomplished
Joint Tenancy with the right to survivorship	In this situation, people will own shares in a property. If one dies, the other person will automatically take over the shares. If both partners die at the same time, then this issue will be back in probate court. You need to be careful in this type of arrangement; if you give someone part ownership in your property, it is irrevocable. They can do as they please with their share of the property. Depending on the local laws and the amount of the share of the property, you may have to file a gift tax return. Sometimes, it can create disputes to have a co- owner after the original owner dies. The new owner can claim that all the assets are then theirs. If this is your intention, then add it to your portfolio. You should check your state laws to make sure that a joint tenancy does not have certain rules or restrictions. You should not step lightly into this kind of agreement.
Tenancy by the Entirety	This is similar to joint tenancy, but is only available to husband and wife. This is only available in some states. You can check with your lawyer or financial professional to see whether this may be an option. The property in this case is transferred from spouse to spouse without having to go through probate.
Community Property with right of survivorship	In this situation, husband and wife have ownership through community property of their marriage. Since this is the case, they do not have to go through probate court. This option is only available in Wisconsin, Nevada, California, Arizona, and Alaska.

> There are some situations where probate may be preferred. One such situation is when you know that your family will fight over assets and are a very contentious family. In that situation, you actually might prefer a court to probate your estate so that there won't be any arguments, or any arguments could be settled by the court during probate.
>
> Gabriel Cheong, Esq., Infinity Law Group LLC

Lawyers

> A good Internet search will turn up tons of information about estate planning laws. The best resource will be a qualified estate planning attorney. There is only so much you can learn and read online, but a good estate planning attorney can digest all that information and create a workable plan for your individual needs and circumstances.
>
> Gabriel Cheong, Esq., Infinity Law Group LLC

You will have to decide whether you want to involve a lawyer in creating your will. It is not mandatory. If your estate is simple and of moderate size, you can probably fill out all the necessary paperwork on your own. The creation of a will usually does not involve complicated laws and practices. The important thing is that you list everything you own and who it should go to. You can even create a Declaration of Trust on your own. You must also re-title the property to the trust. While the paperwork to transfer the title can be a little tricky, it is still something that can be done without an attorney. If you do not feel comfortable doing this yourself, then find a good lawyer who specializes in estate planning. There are some situations, even if your estate is small, in which you should consider hiring an attorney:

- Your estate has a federal estate tax burden placed upon it.

- There are some problems with your family. You may have children from a prior marriage or a child may have a disability. If there is anything out of the ordinary in your family structure, you should consider involving an attorney.

- You have property that may require considerable management or care. This could be the case if you own a business and have not made plans about who will take it over when you are gone.

- If you have signed a marital agreement or prenuptial agreement, this can complicate things enough to warrant involving an attorney.

> The cost of an attorney depends on the size of the estate and the size of the law firm performing the work. I've learned that the higher the overhead of the firm, the more expensive the services. When looking for an attorney, ask people you know who they use and whether they would recommend that attorney.
>
> Jane S Eddy, ChFC, CLU

Attorneys can be costly, charging anywhere from $150 to $400 an hour, but if you have a difficult or complex estate, they will be worth every penny. If you have a simple situation in which you want to write a will but want an attorney assist you, you can probably do so with a minimal fee.

When searching for a good attorney, you can begin by asking around. Your friends, family, and colleagues may have a recommendation of an attorney they have used. You should choose someone to ask who has good financial and business sense. You should also ask people who are over 40 and are going through the process of estate planning as well. They can help point you toward someone who is good and has the expertise needed to get the job done correctly.

You can also ask other attorneys who their recommendation of a good estate attorney is. You can ask them whom they would go to for legal advice in the field of estate planning. They probably know someone confident in the field, or can at least point you in the right direction.

People who own their own businesses are another good group of people you can ask about what attorney they would recommend. Most people who run their own business have professional dealings with attorneys.

If you call your local chamber of commerce, they can give you a list of attorneys in the field that have been solid, long-standing members. Even if they cannot give you the names of estate attorneys, they can probably connect to other attorneys who can make a good recommendation for you.

If you decide to use an attorney referral service online or your local bar association, be careful. They do not always screen or look closely at the attorneys they are referring you to. It is still up to you to assess the particular attorney's knowledge and expertise.

When you decide to work with an attorney, you should write down questions you wish to ask them. Some attorneys will charge you a fee for a consultation, and some will not. Charge a fee does not necessarily reflect on their ethics or practice.

You should ask questions about the following:

- Their credentials

- Their years in practice

- Their years as an estate planning attorney

- Their knowledge about wills, trusts, and other financial concerns related to estate planning

- Their fees

- How they would handle your particular situation

Most knowledgeable attorneys will be able to answer your questions quickly and easily. If they are quiet and not forthcoming with answers, be cautious. If all they want to talk about is fees without answering your questions, then you should shake their hand and leave.

If you walk into an office that looks expensive, then you can expect to pay a high fee. Just because you are being charged considerable money does not mean the person charging you is an expert or is worth it. Many good estate attorneys have modest offices and pass on the savings to you. They know that money is important to you and that you want to pass on as much money as you can to your heirs, not eat it up in legal fees.

Be sure you have a solid understanding of the fee schedule before you agree to hire an attorney. Some may charge you by the hour, some a flat rate for the work, and others will charge a percentage of the assets involved in the estate. Whatever they tell you, make sure that you get it in writing. If there are any extra fees, such as a notary fee, travel costs, or filing costs, make sure you have a solid idea of what the fee schedule for those services is.

The fee for attorney services depends on the state and what the going rate is. The going rate for an attorney in Wyoming is vastly different than that of an attorney in New York City or Florida. Check with several attorneys before you decide to retain one. However, price is not everything.

Gabriel Cheong, Esq., Infinity Law Group LLC

There are basic wills that can be bought at an office supply store, which work well in some situations.

Jane S Eddy, ChFC, CLU

This next set of forms is very important. You should fill them out after you have established your will, and place them in your portfolio. You can also find the forms on the CD-ROM attached to this book.

Will

Here, you will find a copy of my will or the location of my most current will. This section will also have lists of any trusts or special instructions that should be adhered to by the executor or my successor trustee. In addition, if I have any nuptial agreements or property settlement instructions, you should also find them located in this section of my portfolio.

If an attorney or other financial specialist assisted me in creating any of the forms found in this section, I have included their information below. If you have a particular question about a document, you can contact the listed professional.

Title of Document	

When it was Prepared	
Did I have Professional Help?	[ ] Yes [ ] No
Attorney's or Professional's Name, Contact Information	
If the document is not located in this section, where it can be located	
If there are copies of this document, where they can be located	
My Primary Executor or Successor Trustee	
Alternate Executor or Successor Trustee 1	
Alternate Executor or Successor Trustee 2	
Alternate Executor or Successor Trustee 3	
Additional Instructions	
Title of Document	
When it was Prepared	

Did I have Professional Help?	[ ] Yes	[ ] No
Attorney's or Professional's Name, Contact Information		
If the document is not located in this section, where it can be located		
If there are copies of this document, where they can be located		
My Primary Executor or Successor Trustee		
Alternate Executor or Successor Trustee 1		
Alternate Executor or Successor Trustee 2		
Alternate Executor or Successor Trustee 3		
Additional Instructions		
Title of Document		
When it was Prepared		
Did I have Professional Help?	[ ] Yes	[ ] No

Attorney's or Professional's Name, Contact Information	
If the document is not located in this section, where it can be located	
If there are copies of this document, where they can be located	
My Primary Executor or Successor Trustee	
Alternate Executor or Successor Trustee 1	
Alternate Executor or Successor Trustee 2	
Alternate Executor or Successor Trustee 3	
Additional Instructions	
Title of Document	
When it was Prepared	
Did I have Professional Help?	[ ] Yes [ ] No
Attorney's or Professional's Name, Contact Information	

If the document is not located in this section, where it can be located	
If there are copies of this document, where they can be located	
My Primary Executor or Successor Trustee	
Alternate Executor or Successor Trustee 1	
Alternate Executor or Successor Trustee 2	
Alternate Executor or Successor Trustee 3	
Additional Instructions	

CHAPTER 20

Insurance Policies

> Insurance, just like estate planning, varies depending on an individual's situation, goals, and age. To determine the right amount of insurance, you need to look at your goals. Why are you purchasing insurance; are you creating wealth for the next generation, or just protecting you loved ones?
>
> Christopher J. Berry, Esq., Witzke Berry PLLC
>
> Most people should have life insurance that is ten times their annual income, as a general rule. As people get older and acquire more assets, they may be able to lessen this amount. Depending on how congress treats estate laws, people with larger estates may wish to use life insurance and a life insurance trust to fund potential estate tax needs. This needs to be analyzed by a professional.
>
> Rodney M. Loesch JD CFP®, Loesch & Associates Inc.

Insurance is defined as a contract of reimbursement for a loss or injury that is paid on a schedule called a premium. The loss can be property or life, and injury can be to a person or property. The causes can be natural disaster, health, or an accident. The more common types of insurance are health, dental, vision, homeowners, car, and life.

In this section of your portfolio, you should include all your types of insurance, what they cover, the premiums, and insurance company information. This will allow your family to collect on policies, modify them, or even cancel them upon your death.

You may consider whether you have too little or too much insurance. You should review your policies to ensure you have the best coverage for your needs and budget. It does not hurt to shop around occasionally and see whether there are better deals and better coverage available.

You probably have the basic insurance of medical, homeowners, and car insurance. These protect you from things that can happen in life and reduce the costs that can arise from being sick or injured, in addition to protecting your property. In addition to this, have you considered disability insurance? If you are injured or unable to work, this type of insurance can help you support your family and can even supplement government assistance. You should look into it and base your decision upon how many are dependent on your income. Many workplaces offer this type of insurance as a supplemental insurance, and it is usually reasonable.

If you are self employed or own your own business, you should definitely look into buying some disability insurance. If you are injured or become ill, you will not even have sick days to fall back on. If you are not working, you are not generating revenue.

Another type of insurance that business owners have is liability insurance. The costs of protecting your business and yourself from a potential lawsuit are high. It is recommended that you get liability insurance, especially if you are the sole proprietor of your own business. If anything happens, you could lose business and personal assets. Getting liability insurance helps protect all your assets. Even if you are a Limited Liability Company (LLC), you can be sued personally in certain instances of negligence or bad business practices. You want to protect your property and assets, or you may not have anything to hand down.

Business liability insurance will protect your business in the event of a lawsuit for personal injury or property damages. It will usually cover the damages from a lawsuit, along with the legal costs. Depending on your business needs, there are a number of different types of liability insurance.

If a person or their family is depending on earned income, it is crucial to protect that income from loss due to death or disability. For a retired person, if pension benefits will reduce or end at death, that should be reviewed and protected. Depending on the amount of assets involved in an estate, life insurance is one of the best ways to pay estate taxes at a fairly low cost. Long-term care insurance is another coverage to investigate. Some clients feel that they have adequate assets to cover a long-term illness and care, others would rather insure against it. It's a shame to see someone's hard earned wealth dwindle due to medical expenses that could have been avoided with prior planning. Most people prepare with some form of life insurance, but we often forget to protect for disability or extended health care. These are the two that can really devastate a family.

Jane S Eddy, ChFC, CLU

I believe disability insurance for working people can be crucial to maintaining income in the event of disability. Insurance covering the cost of a nursing home or long-term care insurance is a mixed bag, and my only advice here is to be careful looking at these policies to make sure that you are not wasting your money and that the policy will in fact do what you think it does.

Stephen L. Smith, Esq., Horack, Talley, Pharr & Lowndes, P.A.

Types of Business Liability Insurance

- **General Liability Insurance:** This form of business liability insurance is the most common type that many businesses buy. It protects your business from injury claims, property damages, and advertising claims. General liability insurance, also known as Commercial General Liability (CGL), is a type of business liability insurance you may consider purchasing, and in some instances, it may be the only type of liability insurance you need to buy.

- **Professional Liability Insurance:** If you are providing services, such as marriage counseling, you will need this type of insurance. This type of liability insurance is known as errors and omissions. It protects your business against malpractice, errors, negligence, and omissions. Depending on your profession, it may be a legal requirement to carry such a policy. Technology consultants may need this form of coverage in independent contractor work arrangements.

- **Product Liability Insurance:** If you are offering products that you are selling or manufacturing, you should be protected in the event of a person becoming injured because of using the product. The amount of coverage and the level of risk depend on your business type. The level of risk your products pose will drive the cost of this type of coverage.

Life Insurance

For the purposes of this book, life insurance is the one type of insurance that I will advocate you need the most. This type of insurance will pay beneficiaries upon your death. Not only will this investment ensure that your family will have the financial security they need, but the money that is given to beneficiaries does not need to go through probate. Life insurance policies are sometimes purchased to cover funeral costs. The beneficiary takes the funds and uses them to cover any expenses.

> Insurance is a means to an end. Every situation is different, and it depends on the person's income, their desire/need for coverage for a specific period of time verses need for permanent coverage, and their desire for the accumulation of cash value as a supplemental retirement income source.
>
> James F. Seramba, Grey Oak Wealth Management

Term Insurance

This type of life insurance provides coverage for a certain amount of time. If you die during the term of the policy, then the policy will pay out to your beneficiaries. Once the term has expired, the policy also expires.

This type of insurance is cheaper than the other type of life insurance, permanent life insurance. These types of policies are good for couples with minor children, so they may have coverage during the period they are dependent. If you have a business loan, you may also buy this type of short-term coverage. If you die before the loan is paid, the insurance can be used to pay the balance.

Here are some things to consider with term insurance:

- Some policies can be renewable and may not require a medical exam

- Many term policies offer a fixed premium for the first year

- Some term policies offer a fixed premium over a period of years

- Some term policies allow you to turn them into permanent policies

Permanent Life Insurance

This type of insurance costs more than term life insurance, but the policy extends to your death. The only way the policy can end before that is if you stop paying the premiums. Once you have a policy, it will not end based upon your age, health, or age of the policy.

As you pay on your policy, the insurance company will invest your money in an account. That account can accrue interest, which is placed in a reserve account. You may use this account to pay your premiums, or you may borrow against this account. If you terminate your policy, you will receive the money in this reserve account as a "surrender value" of your life insurance policy.

With some policies, you can choose to have the payout to your beneficiaries paid out in annuity payments. This gives a steady stream of cash rather than one lump sum. This may be a good option if you feel your children or spouse cannot handle a lump sum. You can also set up trusts, as described previously.

Under the umbrella of permanent life insurance policies are different categories of policies.

Whole Life Insurance

This type of insurance offers a steady, fixed coverage of the term of the policy. It also offers a standard payment for the length of the policy. The older you are, the lower the premium and the higher the reserves.

> It is my belief that the best kind of life insurance is a Universal Life policy with a lifetime guarantee from a highly rated company.
>
> Mike Kilbourn, Kilbourn Associates

Universal Insurance

This type of insurance also has reserves. Unlike the whole life policy, you can vary the premium and coverage amount during the life of the policy. This amount can change year to year.

Variable Insurance

The reserves that are accrued are invested in securities, stocks, and bonds. This combines a life insurance policy and a mutual fund. This can be risky, as your returns on the investment are linked to a fluctuating market.

Variable Universal Insurance

This is simply a combination of a universal policy, with its variable premiums, and the investment features of a variable policy.

Single Premium Insurance

You pay the premium of the policy in one lump payment up front. It can cost thousands of dollars, but if you are thinking of transferring your policy to another owner, this may be a good option.

Survivorship Insurance

This type of insurance is also referred to as joint or second-to-die insurance. This type of insurance actually covers two people. Both spouses have to die in order for this type of policy to pay off, and even if one spouse dies, the premiums are still due. Couples who are affluent usually are the ones to purchase this type of policy. The benefit is that when the second spouse dies, the estate may owe a significant amount of taxes, and the payout can help defray this financial burden. The premiums for this type of policy are relatively inexpensive, and it is therefore attractive to couples in which one of the spouses may be ill and they cannot afford other types of policies.

First-to-Die Insurance

This is the opposite of survivorship insurance. It pays out when the first spouse in a couple passes away. This is an attractive policy for business partners, because the proceeds go to the partner in the company.

Along with life insurance policies are additional benefits and add-ons. Here are some examples:

- **Accidental Death Coverage:** This can sometimes double the payout. This is often referred to as a double indemnity type benefit.

- **Family Income:** This type of benefit pays out a payment to your family for a specified amount of time rather than handing them a lump sum.

- **Spouse and Children Coverage:** This type of benefit covers everyone in the family. Having this kind of coverage can provide a lower premium, as compared to buying individual policies.

- **Premium Waiver:** This benefit can help you in times when you cannot pay your premium, such as disability. This benefit protects your policy from being cancelled.

- **Renewal:** This benefit allows for your policy to be eligible for renewal at the end of the term policy.

- **Withdrawal:** Some policies will allow you to withdraw money from your reserves. It will reduce your policy coverage by the amount that you borrow.

Everyone's life situation can be different. There are a number of different areas to consider when thinking about life insurance.

- Does your family have other sources of income? If you have a group life policy or some other type of life insurance, you may not need another life insurance policy. There are other sources of income your family may have, such as disability payments, social security, or trusts. You need to decide whether it is truly worth the investment to buy a new policy.

- If you have a large amount of money, you may not need life insurance. You may be better off investing your money in higher yield accounts.

- If you are young, and maybe a little strapped for cash, a term insurance policy may be the best bet. That way, if anything happened to you, your survivors could have access to money quickly.

- You need to consider after death expenses. In previous chapters, I included material about the cost of burial and a funeral. You may have taxes and debts owed against your estate, as well. You might want to calculate what all that will cost, and then purchase a policy that would cover those expenses so that your survivors would not be left with the burden. You must include bank account amounts, securities, and other assets to determine how much your estate may be worth, and then balance that against what your estate may owe. You may be better off with a POD account instead of purchasing a life insurance policy.

- Another thing to consider is covering living expenses for your spouse and children when you are gone. You can calculate how many years they would need the extra money to get by. This can help you decide what kind of life insurance coverage and how much you need to be insured for. Be aware that if you name your children as your beneficiaries, then they will need a properties manager to manage their finances until they reach the age of maturity.

- You may also want to leave money to someone other than your spouse and children. A life insurance policy may be one way to do this. You should decide whether there are other, more practical ways to leave them money.

When you fill out the forms for a life insurance policy, pay special attention to the one concerning beneficiaries. By naming a beneficiary, the proceeds go directly to them without having to go through probate. If you want to leave funds to pay for your post-death expenses, you want to make sure that you name the right people. A successor trustee, executor, or spouse is a logical choice as a beneficiary, as they are the ones most likely to be responsible for handling your burial arrangements.

If you want to leave money to specific adults, you will want to name them on your form. If you name more than one beneficiary, you will be asked to choose a percentage of the benefits that will be paid to each individual. If one of the beneficiaries dies, then you will want to leave instructions on how that should be handled. This can be done on the beneficiary form.

If you live in a state the recognizes community property, you should know that if you purchase a life insurance policy using community funds, then your spouse is entitled to half of the benefits upon your death, regardless of whom you named as the beneficiary. If you and your spouse want to agree to different terms, you need to make sure these terms are in writing.

If you wish to name minor children as the beneficiaries, you need to understand that you will have to appoint someone to manage the benefits until they are old enough to do it on their own. If you do not choose someone, a judge may choose one instead after you die. Relying on a probate court to make this decision can be expensive and diminish the amount of the inheritance. Naming someone ahead of time is a relatively simple process.

- You need to choose a responsible adult who you know have the bests interests of your children at heart. You are trusting them to spend the money for the needs of your children.

- On the beneficiaries form, you can name your children. You then must name the property manager under the Uniform Transfers to Minors Act. You can get this form from your insurance agent.

- If you have a trust, you can name the trust as the beneficiary. Then, on the trust documents, you can name the children as the beneficiaries of the funds from your insurance policy. You can also establish who the adult manager is within the trust documents.

If your estate is large enough, then there may be federal estate taxes levied against it. If you own the insurance policy, then the proceeds from the policy are included. If, however, someone else owns the policy, then the benefits are not included within the estate, and therefore, will not be taxed. You can transfer ownership of your policy to another person or entity to avoid these types of estate taxes. You can either transfer the policy to someone else, or you can create an irrevocable life insurance trust and transfer the ownership of your life insurance policy to that trust. If you wish to transfer your policy, talk to a tax professional or attorney, as there are some complicated tax laws in this area.

Long-Term Care Insurance

This is the type of insurance people do not want to think about, and often do not pay much attention to. Long-term care can be expensive and drain people assets and resources. Many of these policies have specific benefit triggers that must occur in a person's health and situation before benefits can be paid, and there is usually a cap on how much a policy will pay out.

These types of policies can be costly, but if you have enough money, buying long-term care (LTC) insurance may protect your assets. Be aware that LTC insurance is not for everyone. If you are wealthy, you probably do not need LTC insurance, because you will have enough resources to pay for long-term care. Unlike life insurance, LTC may not be a good investment. If you do not have many assets, then there are governmental programs that will likely cover your costs for long-term care.

If you expect that when you are over the age of 80, you will own your own home and have at least $300,000 in property and $50,000 in income, then LTC insurance may be a good fit for you. If you are buying a policy as a way to protect your assets, rather than it being a good investment, then an LTC will be more helpful to you.

When shopping for LTC insurance, there are a number of factors that will affect your cost, such as your age, health, and what benefits you are looking for in a policy. If you are under 50, you can probably get away with paying about $1,000 a year, as opposed to waiting until you are 70, when the premiums can be as high as $3,000 a year. If you are trying to determine whether a premium is within your budget, you should consider a premium that is not greater than 5 percent of your monthly income. If, over time, your rates increase while your income decreases, you may need to re-evaluate the policy.

Some extras you may look for in an LTC life insurance policy are:

- A step-down feature that reduces your premium over time.

- Waiving of premium 30 to 90 days after you begin to use the LTC benefits.

- Policies that state that they will never increase your premiums due to your age. Be careful, because your rates can increase if the state allows them to. Your increase can be 20 to 50 percent over time.

When you are looking at different policies, look closely at the benefits and what exactly the insurance will cover. Some will cover care in the home, while others will only pay for assisted living. You should look for the broadest array of services in a policy. You should also look for how long the LTC will cover certain services, and what the cap is on benefits paid out.

The following forms should be filled out once you have established insurance policies. You should attach the forms along with copies of the policies in your portfolio. You can also find the forms on the included CD ROM.

Insurance Information

This section contains all my insurance policies, beneficiaries, and agent contact information.

My agent or executor should review each listed policy and contact the insurance company to:

- **Claim any benefits due** — for example, medical, workers' compensation, life, or accidental death.

- **Cancel policies that are no longer necessary** — such as medical, dental, or vision insurance, after my death.

- **Modify policies** — for instance, modifying my home or vehicle insurance policies after my death, but before transferring the property to beneficiaries.

Insurance Policies

Type of Policy and Policy Number	Insurance Company Name and Contact Information	Policy Owner	Description of Coverage and Status	Location of Policy
Medical				
No.				
Medical				
No.				
Medical				
No.				
Medical				
No.				
Dental				
No.				
Dental				
No.				
Vision				
No.				
Vision				
No.				
Home and Contents, Renters'				
No.				

Home and Contents, Renters'				
No.				
Vehicle				
No.				
Vehicle				
No.				
Vehicle				
No.				
Vehicle				
No.				
Vehicle				
No.				
Vehicle				
No.				
Personal Liability				
No.				
Personal Liability				
No.				
Malpractice				
No.				
Malpractice				
No.				
Errors and Omissions				
No.				
Errors and Omissions				
No.				
Disability				
No.				

Disability				
No.				
Disability				
No.				
Life				
No.				
Life				
No.				
Life				
No.				
Accidental Death				
No.				
Accidental Death				
No.				
Long-Term Care				
No.				
Long-Term Care				
No.				
Other				
No.				

CHAPTER 21

Automobile and Other Vehicle Information

For many people, vehicles are the most valuable asset they own, next to their homes. It is very important that all your vehicles are accounted for and you have a plan for passing these vehicles to your beneficiaries. There are many different types of vehicles you should consider:

- Cars
- Trucks
- Boats
- Lawn Tractors
- Jet Skis
- Snow Mobiles
- Golf Carts
- Motorcycles
- Recreational Vehicles
- All Terrain Vehicles
- Airplanes

In your portfolio, you should list information concerning whether you have purchased, leased, or are paying off a loan on each vehicle. You should also list where the vehicles are located. There may be other information you need to include, such as marina fees, dry dock fees, or parking garage fees. If you have service agreements, you should include these, along with any maintenance history or warranties.

If you are the sole owner of a vehicle, then you should name a beneficiary. If you do not name one, then whatever state you reside in will have its own rules about whom the vehicle will pass to. If you are the co-owner of vehicle, then it will most likely go to the other owner of the vehicle.

The good news is that most states have mechanisms in which you can pass a vehicle without it having to go through probate. You should check with your state to determine what the best ways are to pass your vehicle to your beneficiary.

If you live in California, Connecticut, Kansas, Missouri, or Ohio, there is what is called a transfer-on-death registration. This document allows the title of your vehicle to automatically be transferred to the named beneficiary upon your death. This bypasses the probate process. While you are alive, you can sell, trade, or even name a different beneficiary if you wish, because the named beneficiary has no rights to the vehicle until after your death. You can contact your state's department of motor vehicles to get a copy of the beneficiary form.

You should let your beneficiaries know they are to inherit a particular vehicle. You may want to place a spare set of keys in the portfolio or in a location designated in your portfolio. Upon inheriting your vehicle, the beneficiary may need to update the vehicle registration, title, and insurance, and will then be responsible for any taxes owed on the vehicle.

If you do not have any beneficiary, you might consider donating the car to a charity or organization that can use the vehicle. There are homeless shelters and battered women's shelters that are always in need of donated vehicles. You should contact the particular agency you are interested in and let them know of your intention of donating your car to them. They may have certain forms that they need you to fill out. Some organizations may not have room or be able to handle a car being donated to them, so you should have a backup plan should your designated charity not be able to take your car upon your death.

Some organizations can also auction your car as a way to raise funds for their organization. Again, you should contact the particular organization and ask them how they wish to handle your donation.

The following forms should contain information about all your vehicles, both owned and leased. You can also find the forms on the CD-ROM attached to this book.

Vehicles

Here you will find information concerning all the vehicles I own. You can find information about where they are located, what is owed on them, any other fees involved with them, and who the beneficiaries are. You will also find information concerning insurance on the vehicles. Some of this information can also be located in section # that deals with insurance policies.

In the case of transfer-upon-death beneficiary, I have included any and all necessary documents in this section of my portfolio with the names and contact information of my beneficiaries. In this case, all the beneficiary needs to do is to take the document, along with a certified copy of my death certificate, to transfer the title. This can be done without the vehicle going through probate.

Vehicles I Own

Vehicle Information	
Make:	
Model:	
Year:	
Vehicle:	
ID Number:	
Creditor Contact Information	Garage or Storage Location
Transfer-on-Death Beneficiary	Location of Documents

Vehicles I Lease

Vehicle Information	
Make:	
Model:	
Year:	
Vehicle:	
ID Number:	
Creditor Contact Information	Garage or Storage Location
Transfer-on-Death Beneficiary	Location of Documents

CHAPTER 22

Debts

If you are like most people, you will have some sort of debt in your life. Even if you are good about paying your bills, there may be some left over after you pass away. I categorize debt into two main categories, for the purposes of estate planning.

Every-Day Debt

These are the bills that we have to pay monthly. These are usually short-term types of debts that people pay. Even if your house and all your cars are paid off, you still have to pay these kinds of debts just to live. Some of these may seem more long-term, but they are items that can never be paid off. They are usually on weekly, monthly, or even yearly payment plans. Here are some examples:

- Rent (if you do not own a home)

- Electric

- Gas (gas used in the home, such as natural gas or propane)

- Coal

- Food

- Items for daily use, such as toiletries

- Phone

- Cable

- Internet Service

- Car Insurance

- Health Insurance (Medical, Eye, Dental — These are never paid off, you have to always pay to keep them active. Life insurance is not included because these policies can be paid off.)

- Parking Fees

- Water

- Garbage Disposal

Long-Term Debts

These types of debts usually take longer to pay. Many of these types of debts can be paid off over time. While you may have to pay on them on a monthly basis, eventually, you can pay off whatever the debt was. Here are some examples:

- Home Loan

- Life Insurance

- Vehicle Loan (can be a car, boat, or any type of vehicle)
- Bank Loan
- Taxes (some of these debts can be paid off and new ones can be assessed)

- Lines of Credit

- Time Shares

These types of debts are not always forgiven upon your death. Some of them will be paid off through the liquidation of estate assets. There are some loans that are paid off, especially in cases of accidental death. Some of the information about insurance policies, vehicle loans, and other types of loans can be found in other parts of this portfolio. The types of debts that should be addressed in this section are those concerning credit cards, personal loans, or other lines of credit.

It is crucial that you list all your debt and credit information in this section of your portfolio. Automatic banks drafts are a wonderful way for people to pay their bills. Unfortunately, there is a smaller paper trail involved, and your loved ones may not know about particular bills that you are paying.

One of the first things you may want to do is access your debt. You should look at your income, how much you are paying out, how much you still owe, and what kinds of interest rates you are paying. You should look closely at all the extra fees that you may be paying. If you are over your credit limit, or are late making payments, you are throwing money away.

You need to also look closely at unusual fees. Make sure you are not overpaying or paying for services you do not need. I have found on a number of occasions that I was not being charged the right amount for services, and had been overpaying for months. It took a few phone calls to straighten it out, but if I had not looked closely, I would have continued to throw money away.

You can save yourself considerable money in late and over-the-limit credit fees by getting organized, paying on time, and getting your credit limits back under control. You will also improve your credit scores, which can bring down your interest rates when you go to finance or refinance a loan.

Begin by reviewing what your income and debts are. This is not a onetime look-over. You will need to look at your finances every month. This may take some time, but you will have better control over your finances and have the most accurate record possible. As you finish your monthly review, you should stick a copy of your financial records back into your portfolio. If anything should happen to you, there will be the most accurate, up-to-date records in an easily accessible place.

You can begin the process by gathering all the documents related to your income. This would be any salaries, dividends, child support, or interest earned every month.

Next, gather all your debts and bills. These should be both long-term and short-term debts. The point is to determine what your total monthly debt is. You can then include incidental expenses like food, gas, child support, or any other debts you would pay in a regular month. Subtract your total debt from your monthly income, and you should have enough to cover bills and a little extra.

If you have a high amount of credit debt, you should begin to use this left over amount to pay it down. Try to make an extra payment, even if it is a half payment every month. You will not only cut the amount of time you are paying a debt off, but you will also be saving yourself money in the form of extra interest that you will not be responsible for.

If you find that you are paying out more than you are making, then you may need some assistance. Here are some Web sites that can help you get back on track.

- **www.Betterbudgeting.com**

- **www.personal-budget-planning-saving-money.com**

- **www.financialplan.about.com**

- **www.consumer-action.com**

- **www.kiplinger.com/tools/budget**

Be careful not to make matters worse by opening up a new credit card with a seemingly lower interest rate and transferring your balance from other credit debt. Many of these low-interest-rate credit cards only remain that way for a limited time. After six months to a year, the interest rate can sky rocket. Read the fine print.

If you plan to use a low-interest-rate credit card, have a firm plan of paying off your debt before the interest rate changes. You will also want to close the accounts of the old credit cards to reduce the temptation to use them again. The point is to get out of debt, not create more.

You can also buy programs to help you keep up with your budget. Some of the ones I have listed are free, while some cost money. It is worth the investment. You can shop around and even download trial versions of software before committing to buy.

- Quicken
  www.quicken.com

- All Purpose Software
  www.allpurposesoftware.com

- Mvelopes
  www.mvelopes.com

- The Other Software Company
  www.budgetadvisor.net

- Visual Money
  www.visual-money.com

Here are some books that may help you budget better and get your finances under control and organized.

- *How to Repair Your Credit Score Now: Simple No Cost Methods You Can Put to Use Today,* Jamaine Burrell

- *The Complete Personal Finance Handbook: Step-by-Step Instructions to Take Control of Your Financial Future — With Companion CD-ROM*, Teri B. Clark

- *How to Get Credit after Filing Bankruptcy: The Complete Guide to Getting and Keeping Your Credit Under Control,* Mitch Wakem

- *When You Have to File for Bankruptcy: Step-by-Step Instructions to Take Control of Your Financial Future,* Matt Pelc

All these titles can be found through Atlantic Publishing, at **http://www.atlantic-pub.com/personal_finance.htm**.

If you find that you cannot handle things on your own, then you may consider finding a good credit counselor. These can be found locally or online. Just as you did when looking for an attorney, do your research. Ask around and see whether anyone has any suggestions. Following are some Web sites that might assist you.

There are many Web sites that claim to help you get out of debt for free, but few things are truly free. Most of the debt consolidation companies will charge you a "monthly fee" for their assistance. Many can help reduce your interest rates and stop the harassing phone calls, but you can also call the companies directly and set up the same sort of plans the debt companies do. The credit card companies want you to pay your debt, they do not want to default or file for bankruptcy. Any amount of money from you is better than no money.

- Myvesta
  www.myvesta.org

- National Foundation for Credit Counseling
  www.debtadvice.org
  1-800-388-2227

- Consumer Debt Counselors
  www.consumerdebtcounselors.com

- Consumer Debt
  www.consumercredit.com

- Family Credit Management
  www.familycredit.org

If you have a question about your credit scores, I have listed their contact information below. You should check your scores every so often. It can affect whether you can get more credit and can tell you who is checking your credit and whether someone may have stolen your identity.

Equifax
P.O. Box 740241
Atlanta, GA 30374-0241
800-525-6285
www.equifax.com

Experian
P.O. Box 9532
Allen, TX 75013
888-397-3742
www.experian.com

TransUnion
P.O. Box 6790
Fullerton, CA 92834-6790
800-680-7289
www.transunion.com

If you find that there are debts that are not yours or need to be removed from your credit reports, you should contact each credit bureau individually. Correcting one report does not correct all three. If you find your identity is being used, contact the credit bureaus and the local police. Below are some other agencies that might be of assistance.

Federal Trade Commission
Identity Theft Clearinghouse
600 Pennsylvania Avenue NW
Washington, DC 20580
877-438-4338
www.consumer.gov/idtheft

Social Security Administration Fraud Hotline
P.O. Box 17768
Baltimore, MD 21235
800-269-0271
www.ssa.gov/oig/hotline

The following forms are designed to help your family members understand your debt situation if you become incapacitated or die. You should include them in your portfolio and update them as needed. You should also include copies of bills and any other relevant information concerning your finances.

Location of Bills

Below I have listed what my current bills are, where they can be located, how much they are, and where they are paid to.

Current Bills

Bill	Location

Automatic Payment of Bills

In this section, I have listed the bills that are automatically deducted from my checking or savings account every month.

Debtor	What the Bill is For	Amount Deducted Each Month	Bank Account and Account Number Bill is Deducted From	Is There a Notice of the Deduction Y/N

Credit Cards

In this section is a list of my credit cards. I have tried to keep it up to date in regards to current balances, which you will find in my monthly budget statements attached in my portfolio.

Credit Card Company	Account Number	Contact Information

Additional Debts

In addition to the bills and credit cards listed above, I owe the following debts:

Debtor and Contact Information	Amount I Owe	The Agreed Payment Terms

Debts Others Owe to Me

These are debts that others are paying to me. Copies of these debt documents are located in my portfolio.

Person who has a Debt and Contact Information	Amount They Owe Me	Payment Terms

CHAPTER 23

Social Security and Other Government Benefits

There are many different types of government benefits that a person can be receiving: Social Security, Medicare, Medicaid, food stamps, or welfare services. There are literally dozens of different types of services, and it is important that you list all the governmental services, both federal and state, that you are receiving. There may be benefits that are owed you or your survivors, so it is important that you let them know what those benefits are.

One of the more common governmental benefits is Social Security. There are different types of benefits that the Social Security Administration pays for the disabled, elderly and their dependents. They also pay benefits to families in which a parent dies and there are minor children in the home.

Everyone who works in the United States pays Social Security and Medicare taxes their entire lives. This is also referred to as the Federal Insurance Contributions Act (FICA). If you work for an employer, that employer must match the amount the employee is paying in and send that payment into the government. If you are self employed, you just send in your portion of the Medicare and social security tax.

Medicare taxes pay for medical costs for people over the age of 65. If you have Medicare insurance, make sure that you include that information in the insurance portion of your portfolio.

Social Security Retirement Benefits

These are the benefits that Social Security that begins to pay when a person is at least 65 years of age. While Social Security pays only about 40 percent of what a person's income was when they were working, most experts would suggest that a person have at least 70 to 80 percent in retirement benefits in order to live comfortably. The remaining amount should come from other retirement benefits from employers and from savings and investments.

People are usually eligible for retirement benefits when they turn 65. If a person waits a few more years, they may be eligible for a higher monthly pay out, which at present is about $1,000. You can also choose to get your benefits at age 62, but the benefits will be less. If you continue to work and are receiving social security, you may receive fewer benefits until you discontinue working.

If you are nearing the age of 65, you may wish to consult with an agent at the Social Security Administration (SSA). You can call and set up an appointment, discuss your options, and fill out any necessary paperwork. You should make sure that you do this in plenty of time before you retire so that you do not delay your benefits.

Social Security Disability Benefits

SSA pays benefits to those who cannot work due to some incapacitating disability. It is the type of injury or condition that is not expected to heal for at least a year and could lead to death. The SSA has its own guidelines that are usually stringent and may be different from other private disability insurance plans. If you have questions about eligibility, you should contact the SSA.

In addition to these funding sources, people who are blind, disabled, or over 65 may also be eligible for Supplemental Security Income (SSI). This is in addition to other benefits and is funded through general revenues rather than FICA. This program is managed by SSA.

Survivor and Family Benefits

If you are receiving retirement or disability benefits, your family member may be entitled to a check as well. The amount can be up to half of what your benefit amount is. Here are the usual conditions for your spouse to receive benefits:

- They reach the age of 62

- Your spouse is caring for your minor child. Your child must be under 16 or disabled and received SSA benefits

The conditions in which your children can receive benefits if you are receiving benefits are:

- They are under 18 years of age

- They are between 18 and 19 and are attending grade school full time

- They are 18 years of age or older and are disabled with a disability that was documented before they were 22

Even if you are divorced, your ex-spouse may qualify for benefits if:

- They are 62 years of age

- Had been married to you for more than ten years before you were divorced

- They have been divorced from you for at least two years

- They are unmarried

- They are not eligible for benefits that are equal to or greater than their spouse's based upon their own work or someone else's

Social Security Survivor's Benefits

For the purposes of this book, these benefits are the most important. These are the benefits that your family could be eligible for should you pass away. Here are the conditions in which your spouse would be eligible:

- They are at least 60 years of age

- They are at least 50 years of age and disabled

- They can be any age and have to take care of your child. The child must be under 16 years of age, or must be disabled and receiving SSA benefits

Your children can also be eligible for SSA survivor benefits if:

- They are under 18 years of age

- They are between the ages of 18 and 19 and are attending grade school

- They are 18 years of age or older and have a severe disability that began before they were 22 years of age

There are others who may also be eligible for survivor benefits, such as dependent parents, surviving divorced spouse, step children, adopted children, and grandchildren. In addition to ongoing benefits, your survivors may be eligible for a onetime payment of $255 dollars to help with funeral expenses. Retirement and death benefits were meant to supplement other types of income and were not meant to be the sole source of income for surviving family members. That is why insurance and investments are so important for taking care of your family after you have passed away.

If you have any other questions or concerns, you should contact the SSA at **www.ssa.gov**, or 800-772-1213. You can also look online or in a phonebook for the nearest branch of the SSA and make an appointment to speak with an agent. Many people receive a yearly statement from the SSA regarding the status of their benefits and potential benefits when they retire. This is a free service, and if you are not already receiving an annual report, you can request one from the SSA.

The next documents have information concerning any social security benefits that you may be receiving or that immediate family members are receiving. This is a good place to put a zippered pocket with your social security card. Many people carry around their card, and this is just not safe. If your card is stolen, someone could steal your identity.

Fill out the applicable sections of the forms and place them, with any relevant documents, in the Social Security section of your portfolio.

Social Security Benefits

I have included all the information concerning my Social Security benefits below. If I die or become incapacitated, it is important that you notify the Social Security Administration immediately, at 800-772-1213. You could choose to make an appointment with an agent at a local SSA office.

Please take the time and review the status of my benefits, and ask the agent whether there would be additional benefits available to me or to my family. You should also ask about the one-time death benefit. You can find information about benefits at **www.ssa.gov**, which is the SSA Web site.

SSA Program Name	Name on the Account and the Social Security Number	The Monthly Payment and Status
Retirement Benefits		
Disability Benefits		
Supplemental Security Income (SSI)		
Family Benefits		
Survivor Benefits		

Other Federal or State Benefits

In this section, I have listed other state and/or federal benefits that I receive. Upon my death or incapacitation, please let the agent in charge of my case know of my status. Please have them review the status of my benefits, and discern whether there might be some additional benefits available to my family or to me.

Program and Contact Information	Type of Program	Name the Account is under and Identification	Monthly Benefit and Status of Account

CHAPTER 24

Bank Accounts

It is a good idea to organize all your accounts and passwords to those accounts. In this Internet age, most banking is done online. If something were to happen to a person, their personal representative needs to know how to access all the online information.

Christopher J. Berry, Esq, Witzke Berry PLLC

Many bank accounts can be set up to be payable on death so that they pass directly to the designated beneficiary. Joint accounts already bypass probate by passing to the surviving spouse, but the payable on death is an alternative to these where you might want to designate children or others as possible beneficiaries. I am also a fan of using revocable trusts in conjunction with a simple will. As long as the person transfers assets into this trust, he or she can get all the assets essentially outside of probate. Real estate does not pass through probate in North Carolina, in any case. I do not think those assets need to be transferred to a trust. The person can retain the power to revoke the trust so they are not really committed to anything during their lifetimes.

Stephen L. Smith, Esq., Horack, Talley, Pharr & Lowndes, P.A.

In this section of your portfolio, you should have the account numbers and locations of all your bank and brokerage accounts. It should include phone numbers and branch addresses and should contain the approximate amounts in your various bank accounts. If you have CDs, IRAs, or any other bank investments, you should have them listed here.

As you are reviewing and including your various accounts in your portfolio, you may see that you want to make some changes. You may realize you have not named a beneficiary, or you may think of a better way to invest or secure your assets.

Should you become incapacitated, those whom you have entrusted to take care or your affairs will have a good idea of what your assets are and where they are located. If they need to manage your bills and estate, they should have access to your accounts. There are a few different ways you can help them take care of you.

1. **You can set up a durable power of attorney for finances. I mentioned this in more detail earlier.** A durable power of attorney gives someone you trust the power to manage your affairs in your name.

2. **You can form a living trust, also mentioned in more detail earlier.** In this scenario, you place your assets in a trust. Your successor trustee can then manage your finances if you become incapacitated.

3. **Joint financial accounts are a third way.** The joint owner can continue to have access to the assets in your account, even if you are incapacitated. They may only be able to pay bills using a particular account, but may lack the power to make changes to the account or to access other accounts they are not a joint account holder in.

If you have a brokerage account, it may be smart to include a transfer-on-death designation. This helps avoid probate, as long as you have named a beneficiary. You can transfer securities, stocks, bonds or other brokerage accounts. You should ask your broker for the proper forms to make a TOD designation.

In addition, you may consider a payable on death (POD) bank account. These are called by different names, such as revocable trust accounts or Totten trusts. You will need to fill out a form at your bank and name a beneficiary to the account. While you are alive, the beneficiary has no power or control over your account. You can do anything you like with the account, such as close it, spend the money, or even change the beneficiary. When you die, the beneficiary needs to provide a death certificate and identification. They will then be given the remaining funds in the account.

If there is a POD designation on a joint account, the funds will be under the control of the second owner when the first owner dies. When the second owner dies, the funds are then subject to the POD designation.

Bank Accounts

In this section of my portfolio, I have placed all the information concerning my bank accounts. If I have any pay- or transfer-on-death accounts I have listed them with my chosen beneficiary's name and contact information. The beneficiary will need my death certificate and some form of picture identification in order to access the funds I left in my accounts.

Bank or Financial Institution		
Account Number	Description of the Account	Pay on Death or Transfer on Death Account ❑ Yes ❑ No
Online Access Information	Debit Card Pin Number	Approximate Amount in Account

Bank or Financial Institution		
Account Number	Description of the Account	Pay on Death or Transfer on Death Account ❑ Yes ❑ No
Online Access Information	Debit Card Pin Number	Approximate Amount in Account

Bank or Financial Institution		
Account Number	Description of the Account	Pay on Death or Transfer on Death Account ❑ Yes ❑ No
Online Access Information	Debit Card Pin Number	Approximate Amount in Account

Bank or Financial Institution		
Account Number	Description of the Account	Pay on Death or Transfer on Death Account ❑ Yes ❑ No
Online Access Information	Debit Card Pin Number	Approximate Amount in Account

CHAPTER 25

Employment Pensions and Retirement Benefits

You should begin planning ahead for your retirement, even if you are not quite retirement age. As mentioned in the chapter about Social Security Benefits, they only pay about 40 percent of your normal income, and your retirement benefits should make up the difference in order for you and your family to live comfortably.

If you have specific retirement accounts, there may be funds left that you wish your beneficiaries to have. Your retirement funds usually will not get tied up in probate court. Your beneficiaries may have to pay taxes on the money received from these accounts.

In order to avoid probate, you should name a beneficiary on your retirement account. This way, it will go directly to them if you die. Pension payments will also be paid to your named beneficiaries directly, without having to go through probate.

If the entire estate meets the threshold for inheritance tax, retirement accounts can be included in that gross estate value, and therefore, are taxable. If the retirement money was in a pre-tax account, such as an IRA, 401(k), or 403 B, then there may be taxes due if money is withdrawn. In the situation of a ROTH IRA, taxes were deducted when it was funded, and therefore, there will not be taxes due when money is withdrawn.

In most situations, you can name whomever you wish as the beneficiary of your retirement account. There are some exceptions, and they can differ from account to account. Some 401(k) and 403 B plans require that you name your spouse as your beneficiary. This may be true with IRA and profit sharing accounts, especially in states that have community property laws.

Your spouse may have some tax breaks that other beneficiaries may not. Your spouse can take the money they inherit and, without paying taxes, roll the retirement benefit amount into an IRA. If the spouse is younger than the deceased, they may be able to extend the minimum distribution schedule. You can ask your tax professional for more details.

In the forms contained in this section is a place to let your beneficiaries know what retirement accounts you have and where they can be located.

Employer Retirement and Pension Plans

I am listing my retirement accounts and where they can be located.

Company that has the Account	Description of the Retirement Plan	Account Number	Amount Vested in the Plan

CHAPTER 26

Real Estate Ownership

Real estate is a tangible asset that can be handed down from generation to generation. You may have property that was handed down to you, and it is important that you make sure that the lineage of passing real estate down is not interrupted by not planning ahead.

There are many different kinds of property and real estate. There is, of course, the home you live in. It can be a house, apartment, town home, mobile home, boat house, or any other type of structure. There are types of property, such as timeshares, storage space, or a barn. It can be any piece of land or structure that you rent or own. In the real estate portion of your portfolio, you should include copies of documents such as loans, maintenance agreements, rental agreements or any other relevant information concerning your real estate.

There are a few different ways in which you can own real estate. Make sure you have a strong grasp on how the property will be transferred to your beneficiaries upon your death. I have listed some basic information concerning land ownership. You should consult your attorney or estate specialist.

Sole Property Ownership

In this type of ownership, you are the only owner. All the paperwork and deeds have you as the owner, without any co-owner. This is the simplest situation, and you can easily leave this type of property to your inheritors. If you are married or have a registered domestic partnership, then your spouse or partner may be entitled to a portion of the property.

Co-owned Property

In this situation, there are two or more owners of a property. There are a few different types of this kind of ownership.

Common Tenancy

This occurs when two or more tenants own a property together. This is the common way that spouses or family members own property. The Tenancy in Common (TIC) can be owned by each person as some percentage. There is no rule on how much that percentage can be. When you die, you can leave your interest, or percentage of the property, to whomever you choose, but that is all you can leave. You cannot transfer the entire property.

Joint Tenancy with Right of Survivorship

In this form of tenancy, each owner must have an equal share of the property. Each owner can sell their portion of the property if they choose. When one of the owners passes away, their portion of the property will then go to the surviving owners, regardless of what their will might dictate. This type of transfer is not subject to probate proceedings. This type of ownership is created with legal documents that state specifically that the owners are joint tenants, joint tenants with the right of survivorship, or some other similar legal language. Different states have different requirements for joint tenancy, and you should check with your state or estate attorney to make sure that you have signed the correct documents.

Tenancy by the Entirety

This type of ownership is similar to joint tenancy. It has some restrictions in that it is only available to married couples in about 25 states and to registered domestic partners in a few states. There are some advantages with this type of ownership in that it restricts either owner from selling or giving his or her portion of the property away without the consent of the other owner. This type of joint ownership protects the property from debt collectors seizing the property. If you have any questions, speak to your estate professional.

Community Property Ownership

This type of ownership occurs when a couple earns or acquires property during a marriage. This is recognized in community property states. In this situation, each partner owns half of the property. In California, registered domestic partners also can own community property. When one of the partners dies, they are free to give their portion of the property to whomever they please.

There is also a community property with right of survivorship. This is just like joint tenancy in that if a spouse or partner dies, the other person automatically inherits the deceased partner's share. This is only available in about five states, so check with your individual state for details.

You can transfer your property and avoid probate by doing a transfer-on-death deed on your property. This is only available in certain states, such as Arizona, Kansas, Missouri, Nevada, New Mexico, and Ohio. You need to check with your state to determine whether this option is available to you. These types of deeds need to be prepared, signed, and notarized in the county where the property resides, and they must be filed with the county land office. On the deed, it should be clearly stated that it is not to be transferred until death. You can choose to revoke it anytime you wish.

The laws surrounding property and real estate can be complicated and can be different for each state. Before you decide who will receive your real estate after you die, make sure that you can really give it to them. If you live in a common law state, things can be difficult if you intend to name anyone other than your spouse or partner as your beneficiary.

This is one of the areas in estate planning where you should consider hiring a professional who is familiar with the laws in your area. You should place the information in your portfolio concerning your decisions and who your inheritors should contact. On the forms below, you can fill out the information so that they can access it easily.

Real Estate

I have listed all the real estate I own or rent. I have designated whether I own the property as a sole owner or as a co-owner.

Property I Own

Where the Property is Located		
Type of Ownership	Beneficiary	How often it is Occupied
Company that Property is Financed with	Who Currently Occupies the Property	Estimated Value of the Property

Where the Property is Located		
Type of Ownership	Beneficiary	How often it is Occupied
Company that Property is Financed with	Who Currently Occupies the Property	Estimated Value of the Property

Instructions for Care of Property I Own

In this section, I have provided you with information concerning who upkeeps the property. Following are special instructions to help you care for the property listed above. I have listed service providers' information in that section of my portfolio with their contact information.

Location of Property	Maintenance Needs	Cost of Maintenance

Properties I Rent or Lease

I have listed the properties that I own but have rented or leased to others.

Location of the Property	
How Often it is Occupied	Contact Information for Leasing Agent
Terms and Conditions of the Lease	Rental Income

Location of the Property	
How Often it is Occupied	Contact Information for Leasing Agent
Terms and Conditions of the Lease	Rental Income

Instructions for Care of Leased or Rented Property

This section has special instructions concerning the upkeep and maintenance of my rented properties. The list and contact information of the services providers can be found in that section of my portfolio.

Location of Property	Maintenance Needs	Cost of Maintenance

CHAPTER 27

Tax Information

There are two tax systems in this country. I don't mean one for the rich and one for the poor, but one for the informed and one for the uninformed. Isn't it time you get informed?

Mike Kilbourn, Kilbourn Associates

There are tax considerations even after you have passed away. The government will get their share of what you own, even after you have died.

You are only worth 55 percent of what you think you are worth. Estate tax rates (after your exemption) start at 41 percent and quickly work their way to 45 percent. And, the taxes are due within nine months after you leave this world.

Mike Kilbourn, Kilbourn Associates

For our purposes, there are three times when taxes are important: the time leading up to your death, the point after your death, and the point at which property is distributed.

Before you die, if you become incapacitated, your family or designated agent will take care of your state and federal taxes. Even if you die suddenly, your estate will owe any taxes that have not been paid.

After you die, your estate will continue to be responsible for taxes until it is distributed. This means that your family or executor will still need to file your annual income taxes. These are taxes due for any dividends, royalties, or similar interest and income paid to your estate.

Once your estate has been distributed, your family or assigned agent will no longer have to file income tax returns. Your trustee will have to file all inheritance and estate tax returns. Beneficiaries can also file their own inheritance tax forms, if they choose.

If your estate is valued over a certain amount, there may be inheritance taxes that will need to be assessed and paid, and there may be federal and state tax forms that will need to be filed. Most people do not have to worry about paying these taxes because the estate has to be valued in range of millions of dollars. If the estate does not meet the threshold amount, then no returns will need to be filed. The amount of estate tax changes year to year, but it can take almost half of your estate value.

There are ways you can reduce the possibility of being assessed for estate taxes, some of which are listed below:

- You can give a gift of about $12,000 a year without having to pay a gift tax

- Pay someone's bills or tuition

- Give money to charity

- Set up an AB trust, mentioned in detail earlier.

- Set up a QTIP trust, also mentioned in an earlier chapter.

- Set up a Life Insurance Trust. This will allow you to deduct the life insurance proceeds out of the value of the estate.

Be aware that some states also can assess an inheritance tax. They also have a threshold that the gross value of the estate must meet before they will assess a tax against it. Currently, only the following states have an inheritance tax: Indiana, Iowa, Kentucky, Maryland, Nebraska, New Jersey, Ohio, Oklahoma, Pennsylvania, and Tennessee. Most states have a deadline of nine months in which the tax must be paid, but some have shorter time frames. You should check with your individual state for details.

The forms I have provided will help your executor and family locate your tax information. You should also consider having a copy of your last year's return in your portfolio.

Tax Professionals

I have listed the tax professionals who have helped me with my taxes in the past and have prior years' tax returns on file. If you need assistance in filing any tax forms, these are the people I recommend that you contact. I have also included a copy of my last year's federal and state tax returns and any important information that will assist you with filing and future returns.

Name of Tax Profes-sional	Tax Professional Contact Information	What they have helped me with in the past

Prior Years' Tax Records

I have listed where my prior years' tax returns and information can be located.

Location of Records Concerning this Year's Tax Return	
Location of Tax Records From Prior Years	

CHAPTER 28

Other Information

There may be information that you wish to include in your portfolio that does not seem to fit easily in other parts. You can include anything you wish in this section. You can include items such as family recipes, family lore, your favorite joke, or eve your fondest memory. You can include important items like passwords for computers, warranties for appliances, or any other documents or information that might be helpful for those you leave behind.

Once you have finished reading and working with this book, go back to the beginning and retake the test located in Chapter 2. You will likely be surprised how much you have learned. If there are still areas that you do not understand, you can go back to individual chapters and seek out the information or talk to your estate planning professional.

Other Income

I have listed other income sources that did not fit in other sections of this portfolio, but are important for you to know about.

Source of Income	Description of Income	Contact Information

Other Personal Property

Here is a list of items I own and have not listed in other parts of this portfolio. These are special items that may or may not be mentioned in my will. These are items that I have special instructions about.

Description of Item	Location of the Item	My Special Instructions Concerning the Item	Who Should Receive the Item

Property I am Expecting

In this section, I have listed items that I am expecting from other estates. If I pass away before receiving these items, I have listed below how I wish the items to be handled.

Description of Item	
Location of Item	Estate I Expect to Receive the Item From
My Special Instructions Concerning the Item	Who Should Receive the Item

Description of Item	
Location of Item	Estate I Expect to Receive the Item From
My Special Instructions Concerning the Item	Who Should Receive the Item

Description of Item	
Location of Item	Estate I Expect to Receive the Item From
My Special Instructions Concerning the Item	Who Should Receive the Item

Description of Item	
Location of Item	Estate I Expect to Receive the Item From
My Special Instructions Concerning the Item	Who Should Receive the Item

Warranty Records and Product Guides

I have listed information concerning warranties on certain items and where you can locate the product guides and repair records.

Item Description	Item Location	Warranty Location	Repair Record Location	Product Guide Location

Passwords and Access Codes

I have listed important access codes and passwords for unlocking and accessing information and assets.

Item to Access	Location of Item	Password or Access Code

CHAPTER 29

Storage and Keeping Records Safe

It is crucial that you choose a safe place to locate your portfolio and all your important documents. Some common places are safety deposit boxes, home safes, and with family or friends. It is important that they have protection against nature, fire, theft, or other disasters.

Storage Tips

Different estate planning experts give their advice concerning the storage of estate records.

> It is important place documents in a safe place. If you do put them in a home safe, make sure to give the combination or key to a trusted friend of family member. Ask your attorney to keep a copy. Make sure to give copies of medical directives to your doctor, local hospital, and the appointed decision maker(s).
>
> Jane S Eddy, ChFC, CLU

Important documents should be stored in one safe folder. These documents should include your basic estate planning documents (wills, durable power of attorney for finances, health care proxy, living will, and any trust documents), mortgage, and deeds, emergency contact and personal identification materials, passports, and emergency medical information. Documents should be stored in one safe place, such as a folder or, better yet, a small, water-tight, plastic box or portable safe.

Gabriel Cheong, Esq., Infinity Law Group LLC

I recommend to my clients that they store their documents in a fireproof safe where their personal representative or trustee knows where to access them. To often, banks have not been timely in allowing an agent of the deceased or incapacitated to access a safety deposit box in a timely manner without judicial intervention. Therefore, I do not recommend they store the documents at the bank.

Christopher J. Berry, Esq., Witzke Berry PLLC

A great place to store documents is in a fireproof storage box, near a door where you can grab it on the way out of the house in case of emergency evacuation, like a tornado, flood, or other disaster.

Rodney M. Loesch JD CFP®, Loesch & Associates Inc.

The wills should go in a safety deposit box, in some sort of safe, fireproof container. The powers of attorney should be shared with whoever is designated as the attorney-in-fact, and a copy of the health care power of attorney should be sent to the person's primary physician as well.

Stephen L. Smith, Esq., Horack, Talley, Pharr & Lowndes, P.A.

Storing documents incorrectly is the main problem that most people cause their heirs. In an abundance of caution, people have their wills drawn up, executed, and then put someplace "safe," like a bank safety deposit box. This is a huge mistake, as the heirs have no access to the safety deposit box without a court order, which you cannot obtain quickly. It makes much more sense to have a designated box of papers located somewhere in your house, or, if you are nervous about snooping relatives prior to your demise, at least have your attorney store your will, and have a letter that alerts your relatives to who the attorney/firm is, and where they can be located. Most attorneys will store a will that they have prepared for free, or at a minimal cost.

David T. Pisarra, Esq.

A minimum of two places —I recommend a fireproof safe in your home and your attorney's office.

Barry Friefield, Tax Partner, CPA, Abalos & Associates, P.C.

If you do not tell your family or trustee where they can find your documents, all your hard work and planning will be for nothing. In addition, if you place them in the wrong place, and something happens, your documents could be destroyed. There is some preparation and planning needed ahead of time or your family may not be able to access the necessary materials that you worked so hard to secure and protect.

Safety Deposit Boxes

A safety deposit box is about the most secure place you can keep your documents and portfolio. If you are not careful, you can make it too secure, and your family will not have access to it after you die.

A safety deposit box usually requires a key, identification, a signature, and specific permission to access. Without these items, your belongings can end up being locked up forever. If you are incapacitated, only the co-owners of your box and your designated agent can access your box. Your agent can only manage your box if they are granted specific power to in the durable power of attorney. I you do not have co-owners or an authorized agent, then the box cannot be accessed without a court order.

After you die, the question of who can open the box depends on your state's laws. In some states, a designated agent or co-owner can access the box without difficulty. In other states, the box can be sealed until the state tax authority assesses the value of the contents of the box. This can take some time. You need to be sure that your trustee or family can access your box before you place your portfolio or other necessary documents in it.

If the box is not sealed, there are a few different situations to consider. Even if you have a co-owner who has easy access to the box, you may want to consider putting burial arrangement information in another safe place in case the bank is closed for a holiday or weekend.

If you do not have a co-owner, and the box is not sealed, the trustee should be able to access your box with a certified copy of your death certificate. This can take a little time, so again, you should consider placing a copy of your portfolio or other immediately necessary instructions in another secure location.

Following are forms for information about where your safe deposit boxes are located and where your safety deposit box key is located. In addition, if there are other secure places where you have placed documents, you can fill out the forms with information concerning these locations. You may want to place your key in a zippered pouch in your portfolio, as long as you do not intend to locate your portfolio in your box.

Safety Deposit Box

Below, you will find information concerning my safety deposit boxes and where to locate the keys.

Location of Safety Deposit Box	Location of the Key

The form below contains information about other locations I have placed important documents and how to access those documents. This can include safe boxes, wall safes, or other secure locations.

Document	Location of Document	How to Access the Document

CHAPTER 30

Conclusion

Your portfolio can be the greatest gift you leave behind for your family. It can take time to create, but the time you save your family later is priceless. You may even find that you want to create a portfolio for other family members or those you care for. It can be a wonderful gift to them. No one really wants to think about death or that some day when they may become incapacitated, but death is inevitable. Some people can be superstitious that if they plan for their estate, they will die soon after. All the professionals that I have interviewed have said that has never happened. What they do all agree upon is that those people who do not plan for their estate often leave an expensive, heart breaking mess behind.

The CD-ROM that is attached to this book contains all the forms you can see here. You can fill them out, change them, save them on your hard drive, or print them out and create a portfolio of your own. They are simple and basic, as each person's life circumstance is different. The forms are flexible enough to be altered to your needs and those of your family. You may also find that some of the sections and forms do not apply to your situation, which is perfectly fine. Create a portfolio that fits your needs.

You do not have to limit yourself to making alterations once a year, as your circumstances can change more often than that. Do not put off making necessary changes, as you may forget, and if anything happens in the meantime, your family may not have the most accurate, up-to-date information.

It cannot be stressed enough that the forms and material contained in this book are not a replacement for an attorney or estate planning expert. What it does provide is a blueprint or frame to gather the necessary materials and documents that might be needed in the estate planning process. Even if you hire an attorney, being organized can save time, and time equals money.

Case Studies

In this section, you will find case studies of experts in the field of estate planning. They are from many different places around the United States and offer their tips and expertise to help your estate planning run smoother. You can also contact the various experts for further advice and help along the way.

The Complete Guide to Organizing Your Records for Estate Planning: Case Studies

Jane S. Eddy, ChFC, CLU
533 N. Nova Rd, Suite 213B
Ormond Beach, FL 32174
386-671-7399

I have found that people who do not get their estate in order can pay unnecessary estate taxes, and legal fees may be paid and assets may transfer to the wrong person (i.e., ex-spouse); unnecessary time will be spent trying to sort things out, and anguish and stress will mount during a time that is extremely emotional.

Estate planning ties things up and organizes your estate to be distributed as you choose. If done correctly, it should be distributed and transferred without too much confusion. For many people, becoming incapacitated or dying is not something they want to think about.

The Complete Guide to Organizing Your Records for Estate Planning: Case Studies

It turns dying into more of a reality. People are funny about it. I have one client whose wife has signed her updated will, but her husband still hasn't gotten up the nerve to sign it. It's been six months. Silly, but very true.

I had one client's husband who was a retired physician. Two items created problems for us. First, when he retired, the Keyman life insurance policy never had the beneficiary changed. The wife paid the premiums, but the beneficiaries were still the three other doctors. Second, the practice pension plan documents couldn't be located, so the beneficiary could not be verified. This was an unnecessary involvement of an attorney due to an oversight. That is why it is important to make sure you have all the details of your estate in order.

Gabriel Cheong, Esq.
Infinity Law Group LLC
One Adams Place
Suite 400
Quincy, MA 02169
Tel.: (617) 273-5110
www.infinlaw.com

I am an estate planning and family/divorce attorney. I have my own firm that concentrates on just those two areas of law. I have had my firm for a year in November. I have been an attorney for just as long. Prior to getting my attorney license, I worked at various places, including a legal aid clinic that helps victims of domestic violence have access to the courts, and also a small firm where I practiced family law and estate planning work. I hold a BS in Computer Science and a BA in Mathematics. In addition, I hold a Juris Doctor (JD) from Northeastern University. For a more complete biography, please visit my Web site at **www.infinlaw.com** or look up my profile on **www.avvo.com**.

Estate planning is so important because it's planning for one of the few inevitable situations in life — death.

The Complete Guide to Organizing Your Records for Estate Planning: Case Studies

A good estate plan also plans for incapacity and the unknown. People are afraid to talk about incapacity and death. It is a kind of taboo in our society. However, as the saying goes, death and taxes are the only sure things in life and estate planning addresses both those issues. The older we get, the more responsibilities we have and the more people rely on us. The most responsible thing to do is to plan for ourselves and the ones who depend on us for when we are no longer there to provide or to look after them.

The most important thing I tell any clients is that everyone over the age of 18 needs a basic estate plan (i.e., a will, durable power of attorney, health care proxy, and living will). If you don't have a will or trust in place, your beneficiaries can incur estate taxes or your property might not go to the person you wish it to. If you don't have a health care proxy or living will, you might get or be denied medical treatment contrary to your wishes or beliefs. If you don't have a durable power of attorney, your family could be hit with huge bills that they cannot pay for.

The question of whether one person can take care of all of your estate needs depends on the individual and their family. Sometimes, one person handling everything is more efficient. However, in contentious family situations, you might want to share that power between two or more individuals so you create a system of checks and balances. Above all else, the person or people you choose to be your executor or attorney-in-fact must be a person whom you trust completely and entirely.

I believe that when a child turns 18, the parents should at least have the child execute a durable power of attorney, health care proxy, and living will. Many kids that age go away to college, and without those medical documents, it makes it harder on the parents of an 18-year-old person to make medical decisions for them if anything were to happen in college or if they're away from home.

The Complete Guide to Organizing Your Records for Estate Planning: Case Studies

When choosing an attorney, it is important that you feel comfortable with them. It doesn't matter if the attorney has 30 years of estate planning experience; if you don't feel comfortable with them or how they're treating you, then it's not worth your time or money to retain that attorney. Experience is important, but more important than experience is knowledge in the field. Experience does not necessarily equate to knowledge. Some younger attorneys actually have a better understanding of estate laws because they're more up to date on the new theories and new concepts than more experienced attorneys who have not kept up with the evolving area of law.

Life insurance should be purchased only when there's a need for it. A person only has need for life insurance when they have dependents. Parents should have life insurance for only as long as their kids are young and unemancipated. If you are taking care of an elderly parent, you might want to have limited insurance in case you pass before your parents.

A new creature of the insurance industry is long-term care insurance. Generally, people around age 55 should start to invest in long-term care insurance. Depending on the policy, it can cover costs of prescriptions and home health care and might allow you to stay in your home when you get elderly instead of going to a nursing home.

In terms of life insurance, most people only need term life insurance. Don't be fooled into getting whole life or universal life insurance, in most cases. Insurance salesmen get paid much more for selling whole and universal life than they do term life insurance, so even though the majority of people only need term life insurance, they will try to sell whole life or universal life.

The Complete Guide to Organizing Your Records for Estate Planning: Case Studies

James F. Seramba, CIMA CFP MBA
Grey Oak Wealth Management
701 Green Valley Road, Suite 304
Greensboro, NC 27408
336.273.9200 office
336.273-7070 fax
336.549-7014 cell
jim@greyoakwm.com
www.greyoakwm.com

I believe people put off estate planning because of the fear of their own mortality, not wanting to deal with unpleasant subjects, being just too busy with all of life's other demands, and not wanting to confront tough, perhaps hurtful decisions.

It has been my experience that if you do not do estate planning, you can incur unnecessary legal expenses, pay easily avoided estate taxes, cause a great deal of stress for the surviving family members, not have your final wishes carried out, have personal property/heirlooms go to people to whom the gift was not intended, have ex-spouses receive unintended inheritances, disinherit people unintentionally, and cause considerable family friction.

In keeping up with your estate, you should have the following:

- an up-to-date will;

- all trust documents; powers of attorney — both health care and durable;

- information on all insurance policies, including agents' contact information;

The Complete Guide to Organizing Your Records for Estate Planning: Case Studies

- statements from all brokerage accounts with appropriate contact information;

- information on employer-sponsored, qualified plan accounts, including statements;

- banking information (both assets and liabilities);

- property deeds;

- physician information;

- an inventory of personal property and to whom it should go;

- funeral arrangements or desires;

- guardianship desires written out.

This saves considerable heartache later. If a business owner, include buy-sell agreements that are in place, as well as CPA's name.

In keeping up with all of this important information, originals should be in safety deposit box with a scanned copy online in a password protected vault (we use E-Money's vaulting technology) and a copy at the client's residence in a fire/water proof box. I believe estate planning should begin when a person is a young adult and then be frequently updated as life circumstances or laws change. I review my client's plan every three years.

I recommend that people have two people designated to settle their affairs, just in case one is unable or unwilling to do so at the time.

It is important to let these people know ahead of time as well and get their consent to being so designated.

The Complete Guide to Organizing Your Records for Estate Planning: Case Studies

It also avoids squabbling later amongst family members. Finally, it provides a natural set of checks and balances.

There are times in which a person may need professional help, such as if you have a complex estate, own a business, have a high net worth, have guardianship issues, and/or have a complex family situation. Attorneys and Certified Financial Planners (CFPs) can help you make informed choices that will save you considerable money and grief in the long run. When looking for an attorney, make sure that they :

- are board certified,

- specialize in this area of the law (not a general practitioner),

- are part of a multi-discipline firm so they can get support from other attorneys as required,

- give a free initial consultation,

- develop an engagement letter that lays out in detail what they will do and for how much that you sign before they start,

- have been practicing at least seven years,

- have a good reputation in the community.

The fees an estate attorney charges depend on the complexity of the situation. I find $250 to $300 per hour standard, so a relatively straight forward engagement would be between $2,000 and $3,500.

The Complete Guide to Organizing Your Records for Estate Planning: Case Studies

Mike Kilbourn, CLU, ChFC, CCIM, MBA, AEP, CAP, CASL

KilbourneAssociates.com
Disinherittheirs.com
Floridadomicilehandbook.com
(239)-261-1888

I have been in financial services since about 1973. In the first 25 years of my career, I was a commercial Realtor, educator (part time), Registered Representative, and the director of a Saving & Loan Company, Syndicator. In 2001, I moved from Michigan to Florida and have focused on Financial and Estate Planning. I have authored and coauthored a total of seven books on estate planning, charitable giving, financial planning, and Florida domicile. I am in the process of writing another book, entitled Enduring Values; Living Legacies.

People often neglect to get their estate in order because of denial, fear, or procrastination. I believe that a person should begin to get their estate in order when they have a significant amount of assets. They should get their will, trusts, life insurance policies, lists of assets, and other financial statements together. People should prepare in advance with a revocable living trust, and having medical directives is a must. If a person owns their own business, they should make sure that they have a succession plan and life insurance in place.

While creating your estate documents, you should name one trustee and have several backup trustees in place. If you decide to involve an attorney, make sure that they specialize in estate law. They should be board certified in trusts, wills, and estates. Typically, estate lawyers will charge between $2,000 and $3,000 to assist you with getting your estate together.

The Complete Guide to Organizing Your Records for Estate Planning: Case Studies

Christopher J. Berry, Esq.
Witzke Berry PLLC | Estate & Business
Planning Lawyers
3883 Telegraph Rd.
Ste.207
Bloomfield Hills, MI 48302
Phone: (248) 971-1700
Fax: (248) 971-1703
Email: chris@witzkeberry.com
Web: **www.witzkeberry.com**
Blog: **www.estateplannning-mi.com**

I am an estate and business planning lawyer. I do not handle divorces, criminal cases, or bankruptcies. I only help families protect their businesses and loved ones. I have been practicing for four years exclusively in my area of practice. I have following the credentials:

- Estate Planning and Probate Section of State Bar of Michigan

- Completed Estate Planning and Probate Certificate Program through the State Bar of Michigan and the Institute of Continued Legal Education

- Member of WealthCounsel, a premier national collaborative of Estate Planning Attorneys

- J.D. w/ a Corporate Concentration from Michigan State University College of Law

- B.S. in Finance & Psychology from Grand Valley State University

The Complete Guide to Organizing Your Records for Estate Planning: Case Studies

While procrastinating with estate planning is easy for most to do, it is one of the most important financial steps a responsible adult can make. Unfortunately, nearly 70 percent of adults have failed to take this step. There are tons of possible problems. Just look at some of the celebrity estate plans that have led to court battles or battles in the media, such as Anna Nicole, Heath Ledger, and Marilyn Monroe. If you do not plan ahead, the courts will make a plan for you. No one wants their affairs battled in open court where anyone could make a claim to their estate, their guardianship if incapacitated, or to parent their children if they pass before making the necessary provisions.

It is easy to procrastinate getting an estate organized for a few reasons. First, talking about one's passing is not easy or enjoyable to think about. That is just one of the many emotions estate planning stirs up. Second, there are very tough decisions involved. For example, if I have minor children, who will plan for their care? These tough decisions can be debilitating to the decision-making process. The third reason people procrastinate is that they think that if they do an estate plan, that means it's their time to go. I actually had a client who put off her estate planning for six months because, she said, "if I signed my estate plan, that means I was ready to die."

Estate planning is important because done right, it is the only way to handle the last years of one's life or incapacity with dignity while maintaining control of one's affairs and assets to pass them to the ones they want with as little legal, administrative, and tax cost as possible.

At the very least, an individual needs a will, health care power of attorney, and financial power of attorney. This would cover an individuals health care and financial decisions if they were incapacitated and their dispositive decisions upon passing. Additionally, a living trust is also a crucial addition to the foundational documents.

The Complete Guide to Organizing Your Records for Estate Planning: Case Studies

The answer to the question of whether one person should be appointed to manage the estate really depends on the family dynamic. Each family is different. The advantage of having one person handle all the affairs and roles in an estate plan is that they are intimately involved in each aspect of the administration. That is, they are aware of both the financial and health care related affairs of the person making the estate plan. Additionally, things can get accomplished quicker if one person handles the affairs as opposed to having to consult others. The downside is that there is no check and balance as they are making decisions, especially on investments.

A person should begin the estate planning process upon reach the age of majority. In Michigan, a person is an adult at age 18. At the very least, they need to have their healthcare directives and financial power of attorney documents done at this age.

A person should definitely involve an attorney in the process — not just any general practice attorney, but one focusing on estate planning. There is more to the process than just preparing the documents. There are difficult decisions that rely on many factors in how to fund a trust in an estate plan, how to handle distribution, how to draft the documents properly, and what tax effects certain distributions will have.

A person should look to experience, areas of practice, and memberships of an attorney. Then, also sit down with an attorney to make sure you are comfortable with him or her. A person should seek out an attorney that focuses on estate planning. They should not use a general practitioner. Estate planning is too complex of an area of law that is constantly changing for an attorney to dabble in it. The cost of having an attorney work on your estate planning depends on the complexity of the estate plan. Estate plans are not one-size-fits-all documents. They need to be crafted to the individual. Generally, fees range from $750 to upwards of $3,500, depending on complexity.

The Complete Guide to Organizing Your Records for Estate Planning: Case Studies

An example of why estate planning is so vital is a case I am handling that is in probate now where the family would have been better served by using a fully funded, revocable trust instead of just a will-based plan. Because the deceased created only a will, his estate went through probate. Unfortunately, the personal representative, who lives out of state, has the added stress of having to go through an extended court process as we go through probate. A trust would have settled the deceased's estate much quicker and for less cost.

A person should have their documents prepared and reviewed by a lawyer every few years. Just within the last five years, there have been changes in the laws that could make older health care directives less effective. Additionally, a person should have their directives in their primary physician's file.

Steven J. Maffei
Attorney at Law
544 Bay Ridge Parkway
Brooklyn, NY 11209
718-491-9397

I believe that people should begin to think about their estate as soon as they come into any assets that they would like to leave to another generation, or when a life-changing event takes place, such as a marriage, birth of a child, or death in the family. A person's wishes may not be carried out if they do not leave explicit instructions. Most states already have laws that dictate how property will be distributed if a person does not leave a will. In most cases, a person's assets would be left to certain family members, and if there are no family members, the money would go to the state.

If you do not plan ahead, you will not be able to determine who would be in charge of your minor children if you should die.

The Complete Guide to Organizing Your Records for Estate Planning: Case Studies

There are tax planning tools that can be used while you are alive and can save your estate significant taxes and fees in administering your estate. If you fail to plan, you will not be able to take advantage of these financial saving devices, and therefore, will leave less money to your beneficiaries.

When planning for your estate, you should think like the person who will be in charge of wrapping up your affairs once you are gone. When a person dies, an administrator or executor will have to piece together their financial picture based on the records they can find. If instructions are left as to the location of your assets and the financial institutions together with statements, it will make the job of wrapping up your affairs much easier. You should begin with all of your financial records and your Will and any Trust documents.

It can be tricky knowing whether to choose one person to handle your estate. It depends on who the person is. If the person is someone you trust completely, and this is the only person you can deal with, I would suggest using that person. Otherwise, I think it would be wise to have several different people handling your affairs. For example, you can have a professional trustee, such as a bank, administer any trusts you may leave after you are gone.

When it comes to storing your estate documents, I would suggest buying a fire-proof box and storing it in a safe place other than a bank safety deposit box. Once a person dies, a safety deposit box is locked and must be opened by the Internal Revenue Service and the contents of that box inventoried. If all of your instructions are in a box in the bank, it may take some time before the box is opened, and any instructions that you may have, such as for your funeral, would not be carried out because no one would be able to get to them. You should also let someone know where the documents are being stored.

I believe that estate planning is important because it is the last way you can care for your loved ones.

The Complete Guide to Organizing Your Records for Estate Planning: Case Studies

By using various tools and techniques, you can assist your loved ones as if you were still alive. Estate planning helps maximize that amount of assets your estate leaves to your loved ones, reduces costs and taxes associated with your estate, and can help to replace wealth that is lost to taxes and expenses.

Some people feel that estate planning is not necessary because their intentions are so obvious and clear. This is wrong. Even though everyone knows who should get your money, the laws of your state may not necessarily agree with you if you die without a will. For example, in New York, if you die without a Will, your spouse does not automatically receive all of your assets if you have children. Many people do not know this, and therefore, die without a Will with a percentage of their estate, which they intend to go to their spouse, going to their children. People also feel that estate planning for may accelerate their mortality. They do not want to make relatives worry that something is wrong and have them wonder why they are making plans about their estate at this particular time.

You need an attorney because the estate and tax laws are always changing, and you need someone who is familiar with these laws. In addition, you have to be aware if there are any other ramifications to your estate planning decisions. Are there tax implications? Do I lose control of the asset while I am alive? A good attorney will be able to give you a complete picture of the consequences of your decision. You should tell your attorney what you want done, and the attorney should be able to develop the plan to achieve your objectives.

Look at the attorney's experience in representing clients in your situation. Can the attorney explain things to you so that you understand what is being done? Are you getting a complete estate plan? Are you given options, or are you being squeezed into the same plan the attorney developed for everyone? There is no universal price range.

The Complete Guide to Organizing Your Records for Estate Planning: Case Studies

Legal fees in places like New York may be higher than in other parts of the country. The fee should be based on the amount of work to be performed.

Glenn A. Jarrett, Esq., CFP®
Jarrett Law Office, PLC
1795 Williston Rd., Suite 125
So Burlington, VT 05403
802-864-5951
glenn@vtelaw.com
www.VermontEstatePlanning.com

I practice estate planning and elder law, including wills, trusts, probate and trust administration, Medicaid planning, and special needs planning. I have been practicing law for 35 years and have practiced in my current concentration exclusively for the last six to seven years. I am a Certified Financial Planner™ licensee and have presented and attended many professional education seminars.

It has been my experience that not getting your affairs in order leaves things in a mess, which can severely hamper your loved ones from being able to obtain income during your incapacity or after your death. In addition, if no one knows what you have, when will they know if they've found everything? It's a good idea to organize your valuable documents and financial information to leave a road map for your power of attorney agent or personal representative.

The purpose of estate planning is to put advance planning in place so that in the event of sudden incapacity or death, things are in order, and steps can be taken by the people tasked with

The Complete Guide to Organizing Your Records for Estate Planning: Case Studies

doing things to make sure the deceased or incapacitated person's affairs are handled quickly, efficiently, and in the way the person would have wanted. There are a few reasons that people do not get their estate planning done. They procrastinate; are in denial, thinking nothing bad will happen to them; or they don't know what to do.

A will should:

- identify who a person's spouse and children are;

- identify anyone they are disinheriting, if a close relative;

- name a Personal Representative (Executor) and at least one alternate;

- create trusts for minor children and for any special needs beneficiaries;

- name people or charities to inherit if all close relatives are deceased;

- give the Personal Representatives the necessary powers to handle the estate.

It is important to hire an attorney for certain tasks. If you don't, you won't know whether your documents will work until it's too late. An estate attorney is someone who is a good listener, is empathetic, and can give a realistic assessment of the matter. You should ask your potential attorney some questions. Will the attorney be available for questions after the engagement is done?

Will there be a fee for answering questions?

The fee for a good estate attorney depends on many factors — the complexity of the situation, the skill required, and the time available to do the work — is it an emergency?

The Complete Guide to Organizing Your Records for Estate Planning: Case Studies

The lawyer may bill on an hourly basis or on a flat-fee basis, where the fee is determined at the beginning and does not change. Generally, probate work must be done on an hourly basis, but flat-fee billing will often be available for estate planning documents.

Here is a story that illustrates why estate planning is so imperative:

A woman became my client after her husband died. He did not have a will, so the intestacy laws applied. In our state, the wife does not get all her husband's property. Most of their property was jointly owned, so she became the owner of all the joint property. However, her husband had accumulated a good deal of stock in the company he worked for, all of which was in his name. Under the intestacy laws, his wife would have ended up with about one-half of the stock. Since they had no children, the other half would have gone to her husband's heirs. In this case, that would be his siblings, who had treated the couple badly over the years. By writing letters appealing to the siblings, we were able to convince them to disclaim (give up) their rights in the stock. We also had to convince the nieces and nephews to do the same. It took about six months to get written disclaimers from all involved. If her husband had done a simple will, leaving everything to his wife, it would have been much easier. Interestingly, he had done a "will" with a non-lawyer that was not close to being accepted as a will. He probably thought his wife was protected, but she didn't find out until it was too late that the "will" was invalid.

The Complete Guide to Organizing Your Records for Estate Planning: Case Studies

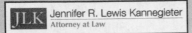

JLK Jennifer R. Lewis Kannegieter
Attorney at Law

Jennifer R. Lewis Kannegieter,
Attorney at Law
jennifer@lewis-k-law.com
www.lewis-k-law.com
(763) 392-1518
P.O. Box 718
Monticello, MN 55362

I believe it is never too soon to get your estate together. It is a misconception that only those with children, large estates, or the elderly should be getting their estates together. Unfortunately, life can be short and unpredictable; we never know when something may happen. Getting your estate together can prepare your family for a difficult time.

To me, estate planning is more about protecting your family than anything else. Experiencing the death or incapacity of a loved one can be an extremely stressful and emotional event. If you have properly prepared your estate plan, your family will be guided through this time. You will have already made many of the difficult decisions, and your family will be aware of your wishes. Your family can focus on grieving instead of being overwhelmed by the process and difficult decisions.

We all experience some ego issues when it comes to our own mortality. Nobody wants to face the realization that we are not immortal, we will die, we may become sick or incapacitated, or we may need someone else to take care of our affairs. To many of us, getting our estate in order confirms our own mortality. It is hard for us to take this step.

Even when we have come to the realization that we will not live forever and we should get our estate in order, it is difficult to place any sort of immediacy on the task. Preparing an estate plan is a

The Complete Guide to Organizing Your Records for Estate Planning: Case Studies

very easy thing to put off; we get busy with life, and we have other expenses come up. I have several friends who have asked me about their estate plans and requested information from me, and every time I see them, they mention the need to get things done, yet they still aren't ready to take that final step.

Health care directives (also known as medical directives, health care powers of attorney, or living wills) are relatively simple documents that can be used to appoint an agent to make medical decisions for you or to give instructions for your medical care if you are unable to do so yourself. In my opinion, anyone over the age of 18 should have a health care directive. Additionally, young adults may want to consider a power of attorney so that there is someone to handle their financial matters in case of incapacitation.

No matter when a person first gets their estate together, it is important to review an estate plan every few years and upon all of life's changes (e.g., marriage, divorce, birth or emancipation of a child, relocation, or career changes).

In preparing an estate plan, all information regarding assets and debts (e.g., titles, deeds, and statements), any citizenship documents, and any divorce or child custody decrees (if applicable) should be gathered.

At a very basic level, a will should appoint a personal representative (or executor) and a guardian for your children, and should distribute your assets in general terms. The will should identify people by name and birth date. Because the property you own can change considerably between the time you execute a will and the time your estate is distributed, a will typically gives general gifts, as opposed to specific gifts (i.e., "I give my car/my house/my estate to ___ " and not "I give my 2002 Toyota Camry/my house at 123 Main Street/my Wells Fargo bank account to ___"). Many states allow for the will to reference a written personal property list for specific gifts. If your state

The Complete Guide to Organizing Your Records for Estate Planning: Case Studies

allows this, a separate document can be used (and updated frequently) to determine who will receive Grandma's wedding ring, Grandpa's train collection, and the like.

If you have not prepared a will, there may be unintended consequences. Your assets may not be distributed the way you wanted. This is especially a concern for people with "non-traditional" or "blended" families. Disputes may arise, and your estate could get tied up in probate for years.

If you have not prepared a Power of Attorney, your family may be required to bring a court motion for conservatorship so that someone else can handle your financial affairs and pay your bills if you lose the capacity to do so yourself. Without a medical directive, problems may arise when your family members disagree on how decisions are made for you, or what those decisions should be. In my opinion, anyone over the age of 18 should have a health care directive.

It is not necessarily the best idea to have one person handle all of your affairs. You may need a person to take care of your medical affairs, communicate with your doctors, and make medical decisions for you if you are unable to do so yourself. You may need a person to take care of your financial affairs, handle your finances during your incapacity, or handle your estate after your death — inventory your property, pay your debts, and distribute your assets. Or you may need a person to raise your children in your absence, someone to provide them a home and deal with their day-to-day care.

In choosing a person to handle your affairs, you should choose someone you trust and who is suited for the job. Everyone has their own strengths and weaknesses. The person best suited to act as a health care agent may be a terrible person when it comes to tracking finances and vice versa. When it comes to children, it is common to separate the financial decisions

The Complete Guide to Organizing Your Records for Estate Planning: Case Studies

from the child-rearing decisions. This allows for a checks and balances system to ensure that your children are being properly raised and their money is being spent in their best interests.

Some people feel pressured to make these decisions based on other's expectations, but when choosing someone to take care of your affairs, spend the time to consider the qualifications and comfort level of your loved ones. If you know your spouse will be too emotional to communicate with your doctor and make medical decisions, consider appointing someone else as your agent (or as a co-agent with your spouse). If your adult child has never before balanced a checkbook and keeps awful records, don't appoint that child as the executor (or personal representative) of your estate.

If there is only one person you truly feel comfortable with handling all of your affairs, then by all means, appoint that person. But make the decision carefully.

You should store your documents some place safe, such as a fireproof, in-home safe. People should be careful about what they keep in a safe deposit box. Banks have certain rules and procedures about access to safe deposit boxes. If you keep your will in a safe-deposit box, your family may have to jump through extra hoops just to get access after your death. It used to be common for attorneys to store documents for their clients. However, we have gone away from the practice as our society has become more mobile.

I have heard too many horror stories about people who have not used an attorney, choosing instead to either do it themselves or use some sort of will-making software or forms purchased online or at a store; these wills then end up missing crucial elements or making unintended distributions. Even with a simple estate plan, there can be complications. I would always recommend

The Complete Guide to Organizing Your Records for Estate Planning: Case Studies

using an attorney in preparing your estate plan. If you take care in selecting an attorney, you will find an attorney to take care of your estate plan and advise you of the various legal implications for a reasonable price. This attorney can also be a source of information after your estate plan is "completed." You never know when your situation or the laws may change.

Find an attorney you are comfortable with. It is important to have an attorney who will take the time to listen to your concerns and explain the law and your options to you. Look for an attorney who does plenty of estate planning work, as opposed to one who does a little bit of everything. There are many different areas of law out there, and in my opinion, it is difficult for a lawyer to keep up on every area. Discuss the legal fees involved to find an attorney you can afford. Ask what is included in the fee and how the fee is calculated. When talking to an attorney, ask what sets him/her apart from the competition. Ask people you know for a personal referral; chances are, if your best friend loved the attorney she used, you will also be happy.

Attorney fees can vary greatly, depending on a variety of factors, such as experience, location, and overhead costs. For estate planning services, attorneys may charge an hourly rate, or a flat fee for services. Hourly rates could vary by hundreds of dollars, and flat fees could range from a couple hundred to a couple thousand dollars. Someone with a more complicated estate should expect to spend more than someone with limited assets and a simple distribution. I would anticipate an "average" price of $500 to $1,000 on the low end. This may seem high, but planning your estate is a way to protect your loved ones in case something happens. Every month, we pay monthly premiums for health insurance, car insurance, home insurance, and life insurance to protect ourselves and our family in case something happens; your estate plan is a one-time cost.

I cannot stress enough the importance of open communication. Death is a difficult subject for people to talk about.

The Complete Guide to Organizing Your Records for Estate Planning: Case Studies

People are extremely uncomfortable discussing their own death or incapacity, and people get emotional when talking about the death or incapacity of a loved one.

But it is much easier to address these issues when you are talking about "what if" and not "right now." Have the conversation with your family now. Talk about the medical treatment you wish to receive (or not receive); discuss how you would want your children cared for in your absence; and let people know your plans for distributing your property. If you are able to have those conversations now, you'll save your family from the shock of your decisions during an already traumatic time.

Rodney M. Loesch JD CFP®
Loesch & Associates Inc.
P.O. Box 237
Moberly, MO 65270
877-505-5101
www.rodneyloesch.com
rodney@rodneyloesch.com

I am a Certified Financial Planner™ specializing in retirement and estate planning and have been doing so for over 28 years. I have a Juris Doctorate degree and the CFP® designation, with the required training and ongoing continuing education.

I believe that people should start doing some estate planning as soon as they are the age of majority in their state (for some states age 18, for others, age 21) because even though you may not have many assets, you always have the potential to have some (i.e., winning the lottery or a law suit). Start with copies of everything you own: titles to cars; deeds to land; and account statements from banks, brokers, and insurance companies.

The Complete Guide to Organizing Your Records for Estate Planning: Case Studies

The biggest problem of not having your affairs together is that the state already has their opinion on how things should be handled (i.e., the intestate statutes on how things are done if you have no will). It may not be the way you wish it would be handled. Without estate planning, you leave your affairs to the law of intestate settlement in your state, and that may not be the way you want them handled.

Maybe you don't want that "no good" relative to inherit your money or property, but the state law may require it. Many people don't want to confront their mortality. Doing a will or trust admits that you are going to die.

A business owner can help out their estate by implementing life insurance applications to help pay to either keep their business running in the event of their death, or buy out their family and keep the business viable.

While probate is less onerous that it use to be, using all the possibilities of transfer on death, payable on death, and beneficiary designation on accounts and titles that allow you to can minimize assets that might go to probate. Here is a story to illustrate how things can be jumbled in court. A family accidently got trapped in probate court over the custody of a surviving child and his money. Joe X, a successful insurance agent, was in an automobile wreck which killed him, his wife, and four of his children. One eight-year-old child survived to inherit a $2,000,000 life insurance policy and the rest of the family's assets. Unfortunately, Joe's will spelled out that Mary X should be the executor of his estate and take care of his surviving children until their majority. The problem was that "Mary X" was his mother's name and his sister's name. The court ending up deciding it was impossible to determine which "Mary" it was supposed to be, so they appointed their own custodian of the funds until the child was 18. Be sure to spell out who you are naming in your will or trust (e.g., "my mother, Mary X").

The Complete Guide to Organizing Your Records for Estate Planning: Case Studies

In most cases, a person should always involve an attorney in will and trust preparation. Many times, their fees are so small compared to the problems that might be encountered by trying to "do it yourself." It only takes one small mistake to make a will void or not valid in your state. Most states have very specific rules, and what is correct in one state may not be correct in another.

A good attorney is willing to take time to listen, and not simply provide a cookie cutter approach to your problem. A good attorney will be willing to return your phone calls and will not dodge talking with you. Attorney fees are quite variable, but most attorneys are willing to have a no-cost, or low-cost initial conference, and at that time can give you a good faith estimate of what you might expect to pay for your project. By putting together a succinct analysis of your assets and liabilities before going to a lawyer, you can minimize the time and expense they have to spend on your estate planning.

Stephen L. Smith, Esq.
Horack, Talley, Pharr & Lowndes, P.A.
2600 One Wachovia Center
301 South College Street
Charlotte, North Carolina 28202-6038
(704) 716-0818
SSmith@HorackTalley.com

I have been working in primarily estate planning and tax work since 1976. I have a subspecialty in IRA and 401(k) investment in real estate, which I found relates very significantly to estate planning. I was Order of the Coif, which means the top 10 percent of my class at the University of Virginia, School of Law. I have also taught seminars over the years on estate planning and other topics.

While you are never to young to start getting organized, it is certainly something that people should think more seriously about as they get into their 50's and 60's.

The Complete Guide to Organizing Your Records for Estate Planning: Case Studies

The key is to make sure everything is in place prior to the time any of their mental faculties may start to lapse or they may have real health issues.

Obviously, everyone should have a will, but a power of attorney covering financial affairs plus a health care power of attorney covering health care issues and life support issues are key. The key items that need to go in a will are as follows:

a. Where the person's property should go. This should cover not only the surviving spouse, but also what happens if the spouse predeceases. For example, provisions may be made for children and grandchildren.

b. The will should also touch upon whether there are any trusts for children and grandchildren so they do not receive their full inheritance at age 18.

c. The will should name an executor who will work with the estate itself, as well as the trustee of any trusts. Backups to the primary designated people are useful as well.

d. The will should also designate the parent's choice of a guardian for any minor children. While the choice of the guardian is not binding on the courts in North Carolina, we have found in our experience that the directives are universally followed, unless the person turns out to be of dubious character or some change had occurred, such as significant drug or alcohol use, that would cause the person to no longer be a good choice.

I think medical directives are crucial, and what is now most effective in North Carolina is a health care power of attorney.

This document not only covers your wishes, but actually designates a person to be able to communicate with the physician and to make sure that your choices are followed.

The Complete Guide to Organizing Your Records for Estate Planning: Case Studies

I think this is far better than the old directives.

There can be big problems, including the disposition of the estate at death, if no will was present, in which case the property would be divided among the heirs based on the intestate succession law. Perhaps just as important is the financial power of attorney, because a person often has a prolonged period of incapacity prior to death during which they are no longer capable of handling their own affairs. Absent a power of attorney, it may be necessary to get a guardian appointed for the person, which can be an embarrassing, expensive process.

A person should look for an attorney who has experience in dealing with estate planning so that they can clearly explain the alternatives available. I think it is also important that you have an attorney who has done this long enough that they are not afraid to tell you when they think you are making a mistake. Ultimately, everything is the client's decision, but a good attorney can at least counsel the client when he or she thinks the client is making a mistake.

For consultations, it is usually done on an hourly basis. For preparation of basic documents, this is usually done on a flat fee basis with the wills and powers of attorney being maybe $500 and a living trust together with a pour-over will being approximately $1,500.

Probate fees are capped in North Carolina. I think that sometimes, people over-blow the significance of probate as a negative. Having said that though, in my estate planning practice I typically use revocable trusts so the assets are kept out of probate. The biggest negative to assets being included in probate, from my perspective, is the fact that the will and the assets become public record. In the case of assets that are put into a living trust or a revocable trust, these assets can remain private, as can the trust provisions.

I think these benefits are even more important than avoiding the cost and time involved in probate. Another real negative to the probate process is the involved in dealing with the clerk of

The Complete Guide to Organizing Your Records for Estate Planning: Case Studies

court's office, and the use of the revocable trust can reduce or even eliminate this.

Life insurance is important at a younger time in a person's life when they may need to take into account an early death. As a person ages, if they are accumulating assets, then the need for the life insurance probably passes, and these policies can then often be cashed in. I think a person would consider leaving insurance in place only if they did not have much in the way of other assets and wanted to make sure their heirs were left in a position to pay funeral expenses and the like.

I think the key tip that I would give to people would be to make sure they organize their records and keep an accurate list of things such as bank accounts, IRAs, 401(k) accounts, life insurance policies, and the like, as well as contact information, including telephone numbers and e-mail addresses so that someone picking up after a person's death or incompetency has an easy roadmap to how to proceed and whom to contact to get help.

David T. Pisarra, Esq.
1305 Pico Blvd.
Santa Monica, CA 90405
DPISARRA@PISARRA.COM
310-664-9969

I do primarily Family Law, but have practiced Estate Planning for the past 15 years. A person's estate encompasses more than just their home; it includes all their personal belongings, including pets. It also references their wishes in regard to how they wish to be treated medically, and in the event of their demise, their disposition upon death.

I believe that all adults, regardless of their net worth, should make their wishes known, if only so that their loved ones don't have to guess at what was desired.

The Complete Guide to Organizing Your Records for Estate Planning: Case Studies

The main documents that one needs to have, before death, are the Durable Power of Attorney, the Living Will, and a listing of all bank accounts. After death, the executor and/or the trustee will need to have a list of the assets and debts and a letter describing what the decedent wanted as their final resting place; it is also very helpful to have at least one bank statement and stock ledgers available to identify the account and financial institution.

People are scared of facing the hard choices that must be made, and many of them figure that they are already gone, so it's not their problem. This is a selfish decision made out of fear. The fact is that making a plan is not that hard, it is simply a matter of laying out what you want to have happen. Some people are afraid that the decisions they make will "offend" their children or spouse; this is where the "after I'm gone" thinking should take over. No one needs to know your plan before you're gone; they just need to know where to get it. You can make your plans with your attorney, who will keep it safe and secret until after you are gone.

Facing our mortality is one of our greatest fears, and yet, it is something all of us must do at some point. If we fail to plan, the state has a plan for us; it generally is not what we would want. Also, failing to plan when there is a business involved is unfair to your partners, and your employees and customers, all of whom are affected by your unavailability, either temporarily or permanently.

The will is really just a listing of who gets what. It frankly is not a place to spill your anger at a rebellious child, or state your long-time hatred of a great aunt Lucille. Just list your children, spouse, what assets you have, and who you want to receive the family heirlooms. The goal is to be as specific as possible so that the executor can make an orderly distribution.

Remember that all heirs are entitled to a copy of the will; this is to make sure that no one "cheats".

The problems of not planning for your estate are endless.

The Complete Guide to Organizing Your Records for Estate Planning: Case Studies

There is the likelihood of your heirs arguing over what you wanted — the perennial problem of "I was promised …" If you have a business, and it needs to have someone put in charge, that needs to be addressed. If you have animals, what is going to happen to them? Properties need to be managed; assets need to be sold and managed. All of this can lead to legal challenges to whatever choices the eventual executor/administrator makes.

This is the situation that probate attorneys love, because it leads to plenty of work for them, in fighting over who should get what, and how it should all be done. There are hurt feelings when decisions are avoided, and brothers have stopped speaking to each other forever over perceived slights, and sisters have hated each other over a "promised" brooch that was never dealt with.

A business that was built over a lifetime can be destroyed in a matter of days if a succession plan is not in place. Your competitors can and will take advantage of the chaos that occurs when a central figure in a company dies or becomes incapacitated. In the case of incapacitation, a person should have a will that nominates a guardian/conservator for their person and for their estate. When someone is incapacitated, they have two needs; one is for their physical person — who will feed, clothe, and bathe them. The other is for their assets and financial state — this is regarding paying their bills, running their company, and monitoring their money.

A person can have one or two people to handle these issues. It is recommended that they know each other prior to their caretaking of the conservatee. They should both be nominated by the conservatee, so that the court has someone to appoint, otherwise, a professional guardian/conservator may be appointed, and they will likely know nothing of what likes and dislikes the conservatee has.

A proper succession plan is crucial to the long-term sustainability of a company. In the event of a death or disability, a company needs to know who will be taking over.

The Complete Guide to Organizing Your Records for Estate Planning: Case Studies

This should be not just a "who's in charge," but also a long-term strategic plan, which includes all the ongoing operations that a President or CEO of a company knows about, but has not told all of his direct reports.

If a company has more than one owner, a properly drafted and funded buy/sell agreement so be drafted. This is so that the other partners aren't faced with having to answer to a grieving spouse who knows nothing of the business. Buy/Sell agreements can be funded in several ways, the most common of which is a life insurance policy that is owned by the company and paid for by the company, which provides the needed money to buy out a deceased partner's share.

In reference to whether one person should handle all of your affairs, my general answer is no. It is preferred to have a point person who tackles all the problems and provides a comprehensive answer, based on the wishes of the decedent, but this answer depends on the size of the estate. A large estate can be a major job to administer, particularly if it involves several heirs, some of whom may be fighting over what their shares are. An estate that has considerable real estate may also present different problems of management. Most states recognize the right of an administrator to hire additional help, so even if one is "in charge," they can still get help.

If the estate is large, or if there is expected to be fighting, the administrator can and should be paid for their services; this will also weigh in on the decision of whether to have one or more people administrate.

Frequently in conservatorships, it is advisable to have one person be the guardian/conservator of the person, and another for the financial estate, as they involve different responsibilities.

For those who truly want to avoid probate, the process whereby the state takes control of your assets and administers the distribution of them to your heirs, your must make a

The Complete Guide to Organizing Your Records for Estate Planning: Case Studies

Living Trust (sometimes called a Revocable Trust), and you must make sure it is current at all times with the listing of your current large assets. Any asset that is above the legal limit in the state of residence of the decedent must have been transferred into the trust, in order for it to be administered in accordance with the trust documents.

For small estates, it is possible to plan around a trust, by holding property in joint tenancy with your heirs. This has its own set of problems, and those cannot be dealt with here entirely.

It is absolutely imperative to have an attorney help you with your estate planning. This is work for a trained professional and mistakes can be costly; also, an attorney can present solutions that the average non-attorney would not think of. If you have an asset base that you want to distribute to heirs, there are ways in which to maximize the value of the gifts, and to minimize the fighting and hurt feelings.

When looking for an attorney, you should be seeking someone with experience and understanding. A good attorney will present options that you have not thought about, and possible problems and solutions that you need to think about. Depending on locale, the experience of the attorney, and the size of your estate and needs, you can expect to pay an attorney anywhere from $150 to $700 per hour. Most trust documents for the average estate, which means a home, a few savings accounts, and maybe some stocks and bonds, should be prepared for around $2,000 to 5,000.

The important, value-added aspect of an attorney is the follow-through, the actual transferring of assets into the trust. There are many "trust mills" that will prepare your documents for you for $399, but that is only the easy part of the process.

It is the actual funding of the trust and the maintenance and education by an attorney of you, the trustor, of how to maintain your trust, that is important.

Buying a trust and not funding it is like standing on a boat in

The Complete Guide to Organizing Your Records for Estate Planning: Case Studies

the desert — it is nice to be there, but it is not being used for its intended purpose.

Be fair to your children; treat them equally when distributing assets. If one has a particular love of an asset, make sure that it is balanced out to the others. Even if you have a favorite child, or more likely, a black-sheep child, treat them equally. Remember that when you are gone, they have each other to deal with, and anything that you can do to continue that relationship is a good thing. If you have specific bequests to make, also present a letter to all your children explaining your thinking and reasoning; it will make the all the difference in the world to them.

David M. Williams, CFP®
Business Enhancement Associates, LLC
8001 Centerview Parkway, Suite 201
Cordova, TN 38018
(901) 473-9000 x206
http://beamemphis.blogspot.com
beamemphis@hotmail.com
http://www.linkedin.com/in/davidmwilliams

I work with business owners and corporations to grow, protect, and distribute wealth. I have devoted the last five years to consulting with businesses and their executives through this firm, Business Enhancement Associates, LLC. I help business owners and corporations grow, protect, and transfer wealth. Prior to establishing my business consultancy, I was Director of Financial Planning for Regions Morgan Keegan Trust.

I have over 25 years experience as a financial planner dealing primarily with business owners. I have developed special expertise in advanced estate and charitable planning, community property and Napoleonic law, employer stock option planning, and qualified plans.

The Complete Guide to Organizing Your Records for Estate Planning: Case Studies

I have been a Certified Financial Planner™ Practitioner since 1985. I was Past President of the Financial Planning Association of the Mid-South. I am currently a Host on AdvisorMax, the independent financial advisor's source for practice management.

A person's estate is not separate from his life. He is putting his estate together as soon as he has important documents or pending events in his life. He needs to keep these records somewhere that he or someone acting for him can find them. While some of these documents accumulate early and may be saved by parents/guardians (e.g., birth certificate, Social Security card, school transcripts, or life/accident/health/property & casualty insurance), the individual becomes personally liable for these documents at the age of majority. Going forward, getting one's estate together is an outcome of being able to function in life.

While young, we believe we are invincible. Death and disability are far off and can be dealt with later, we think. Once mature, we know that time and unforeseen events can happen to us, but it is uncomfortable to think about the inevitable. However, it is important to take care of settling your estate. Documents need to be stored in a safe, access-controlled, accessible place. It is wise to have, at a minimum, a safe or metal box that one can access and carry in an emergency. If additional secure storage is available for permanent storage, then this box should have originals of frequently changing documents and copies of more permanent documents. Originals can be stored in a safe deposit box at a bank or trust company. Electronic copies can be held in online storage services. The key is to have legally acceptable copies accessible, and that someone else can access them in the event of death or incapacity.

If you do not have your affairs in order in the least, if you were irresponsible before death or disability, then state law and creditors will force someone else to be responsible for you. A spouse or heir may not be able to get access to bank and brokerage accounts, and the state may apportion your assets

The Complete Guide to Organizing Your Records for Estate Planning: Case Studies

in ways that injure your heirs and put them under the burden to report to the responsible party (e.g., judge) before they do anything with your assets. For example, state law may say that a spouse gets 1/3 of assets and children get 2/3 of assets. The spouse is responsible to protect the 2/3 of assets for the minors and may be limited in how to spend these funds for their benefit. She would have to make an annual accounting of all income and outflows on these assets, and may be limited to investing these assets in T-Bills or bank accounts.

In reference to the idea of whether to have just one person take care of your affairs, it depends on individual capacity, estate complexity, and trustworthiness. Often, the spouse is the first one considered, and this may be a logical choice. However, it is wise to consider the spouse's functional state after your death or incapacity.

Often, a Revocable Living Trust (RLT) can be established that names a successor Trustee who can act in the Grantor's stead. An elderly gentleman had created and funded (transferred ownership of assets into the name of the trust) an RLT which named his son as Successor Trustee and as a Beneficiary. The Grantor was still mentally competent, and was still driving, but found that keeping track of his finances was becoming burdensome. He elected to step down as Trustee to let his son take care of the bookkeeping. The Grantor decided that he wanted a new car. Unfortunately, the son had taken emotional ownership of his father's assets and did not want to spend money on a car for his father. The Grantor did not get a new car.

In the case above, the Grantor would have been better served if there were co-trustees.

Sometimes, an individual trustee and a corporate trustee are selected. The individual trustee ostensibly looks after the needs of the family while the corporate trustee looks after the needs and wants of the Grantor. In the event that both trustees agree

The Complete Guide to Organizing Your Records for Estate Planning: Case Studies

that an action must be taken that is not acceptable to the rest of the family, the individual trustee can blame the corporate trustee for the decision and not lose favor within the family.

I have seen cases where one spouse has a brokerage account in his/her name only, then becomes incapacitated. The competent spouse cannot make changes to the account or place trades in the account (often it is necessary to go to cash because the owner's incapacity creates major life changes) until the competent spouse has a judge order a conservatorship to give him/her power over the incapacitated spouse's affairs. Some ideas for avoiding probate are the following:

- The Revocable Living Trust allows the Grantor to control and use his assets while alive, puts in place a trustee to act in his stead in the event of death or disability, lists the disposition of assets at death, and avoids probate. One must re-register most of his assets to the RLT for it to work.

- Contractual arrangements such as beneficiary designations bypass probate and the will.

- Certain classes of ownership such as Joint Tenants in Common, Community Property, Totten Trusts, or Transfer-on-death accounts also bypass probate and the will.

An attorney becomes necessary for estate planning as a person's assets become greater and/or his life becomes more complicated (e.g., marriage, children, or owning a business). Estate planning attorneys can apply their knowledge to reduce future difficulties and expenses, and potentially reduce estate taxes. Make sure that the attorney specializes in estate work. The best source for finding a good attorney is through recommendation by friends, family, and/or advisors. Interview the estate attorney and make sure you can work with him/her.

The Complete Guide to Organizing Your Records for Estate Planning: Case Studies

Kim Allen-Niesen
Retired Estate Planning Attorney
www.bookstorepeople.com

I am a retired estate planning attorney; I practiced for 18 years, and now I am a writer. In my experience, a person should get their estate in order, if they have any assets, as soon as they are 18, or as soon as they have assets that do not pass by beneficiary designation, such as a house or stock account, or if they have assets of significant value (more than $1M) that pass by beneficiary designation. If they do not have any assets, then they should begin as soon as they have a child. It could be that in the early stages that the client does not need much more than to be educated and a simple document, but when a person starts acquiring assets or descendents, a talk with an estate attorney is in order.

If you neglect to get your estate in order, you will pay much more in attorney fees for one, especially in a state where a probate could be avoided if you used a revocable trust. If you want your children to be raised by a non family member, that is much more difficult without a Will because the default provisions name family members. Considerable tax planning will be lost if the proper documents are not completed. There could be discrepancies between the various beneficiary designations if they are not reviewed (I had a case where the hated ex-husband received a pension).

It is a responsibility of every person to take care of their family and assets, and that includes what happens to them at death.

Without clear planning, the estate could pay far more in taxes and could cause severe family problems (such as if there are children from a previous marriage), considerable grief, expense, and pain, all of which can be reduced by having a smooth-running estate plan.

The Complete Guide to Organizing Your Records for Estate Planning: Case Studies

One of the reasons people are reluctant to discuss estate planning is if fear that if they talk about it, then it could happen. I told my clients that the only clients who died right after meeting with me were the ones who were on their death bed already; there is no correlation between the planning and the event. It is amazing how many people were superstitious. Plus, it costs money to do something that is largely unpleasant and labor intensive. Who would not rather spend the money on a weekend away?

If the client has assets, an attorney must be seen; the law is too nitpicky for a layperson with assets to work around. When looking for the right attorney, competence and expertise are important; I would only go to an attorney who practices estate planning and administration in at least 80 percent of his/her practice. It is a little different than choosing an attorney for almost any other purpose; the estate planning attorney knows the secrets of your family and your money and hopefully will work with you for the rest of your life, so you need to have a person you are comfortable with, similar to picking your primary doctor.

The cost of a good estate attorney varies all over the place. I live in L.A., where big firms charge $5,000 for a basic plan. When I was on my own, I charged $2,000 for a basic plan that included will, trust, medical directives, funding docs, and beneficiary designations.

I am not a fan of whole life insurance policies unless the person is financially irresponsible and it is the only way he will save money. Generally, a better return is received outside of the policy. However, there are some sophisticated insurance plans that help reduce income tax or through loaning serve as seed money for other investments. Also, if there is going to be a large estate tax, there is a benefit to whole life to estate tax payment purposes. Absent the higher level planning, I favor large amounts of term while the clients are raising children, and when they are gone, then cut back on the insurance. I advised my clients to have insurance in case of catastrophe, but build up their assets so that by the time the kids are gone,

The Complete Guide to Organizing Your Records for Estate Planning: Case Studies

there are enough assets to live on for both spouses without resorting to insurance.

Get disability insurance; it is very important. The worst thing financially that can happen to a family is that an income earner is disabled but does not die (thereby triggering the life insurance); disability insurance covers that eventuality. Supplement employer disability insurance; it is rarely enough.

Be honest with your estate planner. Do not be ashamed about anything in your family; believe me, we have heard it all. Think about whether you want your assets to be held in trust for your children or disturbed outright and who would be the trustee and how would you want the funds distributed. Generally, I recommend that one sibling should not be trustee for another. If you have a special-needs child, see an attorney. Also, think about where you would want your assets distributed if every one of your named beneficiaries died (e.g., siblings, heirs, or charity).

Joseph H. Gruner
Gaines Gruner Ponzini & Novick, LLC
Ono N. Broadway
White Plains, New York
914-288-9595
370 Lexington Ave.
New York, NY, 10017
212-883-6820

I am an attorney involved in estate planning, estate administration, and elder law. I have been involved in this type of practice for over 30 years.

I believe a person should get their estate together as soon as they believe they have enough assets to care who it would go to. A will is really not a place for information, since a good deal of that information is subject to change.

The Complete Guide to Organizing Your Records for Estate Planning: Case Studies

The will should contain the names and relationships of the people who are to receive any benefit under the will; you can also include their addresses, but they are subject to change, and the amount or the percentages they are to receive. The problems that can arise if affairs are not put in order include the inability to locate assets or beneficiaries, additional legal costs, and additional administration expenses.

If a person becomes incapacitated, there is very little that person can do at that time. Hopefully, the incapacitated person already has a durable power of attorney and medical directive. If not, someone will have to bring a guardianship proceeding in court in order to obtain the power to care for the incapacitated person's assets and health.

Whether there should be one or more persons taking care of an estate depends on the people involved and the assets involved. If that would result in too many people, then name three people. Except when it is the surviving spouse, I usually like to have more than one person, so there are checks and balances.

In New York, avoiding probate in most cases is not necessary. If a person wants to avoid probate, then his assets should be held in such a way that there is a beneficiary designation or a pay-on-death designation, or the assets are in a living trust.

In almost all cases, an attorney should be involved, because the documents necessary for proper estate planning, such as durable powers of attorney, wills, and trusts should only be prepared by an experienced attorney to avoid problems when the documents have to be used.

A good attorney has many qualities, including experience, good listening skills, good communication skills, and knowledge of the law. The cost of an attorney depends on how much work is involved and the degree of expertise required to give the advice needed and to prepare the documents required.

The Complete Guide to Organizing Your Records for Estate Planning: Case Studies

Barry Friefield, Tax Partner, CPA
Abalos & Associates, P.C.
7150 N. 16th Street
Phoenix, AZ 85020
barry@abaloscpa.com
Phone: (602) 943-1984 x107
Fax: (602) 943-4669

I am tax partner at Abalos & Associates, PLLC, a full service CPA firm with expertise in the fields of financials, advanced tax planning strategies, profit enhancement, consulting, technology consulting, and life-planning services. I have been doing this type of work for 30 years. I have a B.S. in accountancy from the University of Illinois and am a CPA.

A person should begin to organize their estate the day after they are born. No, seriously – anyone with assets, children, a spouse, or special needs should be looking at getting their estate together. For assets, you need to figure out where these will go. If you do not direct them, the state will. Depending on which state you are in, dying without a will allows the state to allocate X amount of your assets to your child, spouse, or other beneficiary. You want to have control of what happens after you die, and estate planning gives you that control.

Many unintended consequences can arise from not preparing your estate. By not getting your affairs in order, you have lost the opportunity to direct anything after you have passed. This can result in family conflict, the state exercising their power, extra probate, law suits, and guardianship issues with your children.

The Complete Guide to Organizing Your Records for Estate Planning: Case Studies

If a person is incapacitated, it may be to too late at that point to do anything about their estate or affairs. It depends on the degree to which they are incapacitated and what functions are affected. If they can articulate through writing or talking, they have a fighting chance to make their decisions heard.

Have a life planning service. Make a checklist of items, and keep it in a life-planning binder. The list is endless and needs to include everything someone would need to know if you were not able to tell them, including your doctors' names and where they practice. Have you purchased a cemetery plot? Have you made funeral arrangements? Who do your car, bank account, child, pet, or other items go to?

Answers to the Estate Planning Quiz

Here you will find the answers to the questions in Chapter 2.

1. **F** While it does not require one, there are some aspects in which an attorney is recommended.

2. **F** There is no federal law that requires that a body be embalmed. Putting a body in a freezer will preserve it for a few days until a funeral.

3. **F** There is no law requiring you to buy anything from a funeral home. While they offer such items as caskets, you are not required to buy them.

4. **F** You may want to check with local laws, but you are allowed to scatter them in most public places.

5. **F** This allows you to bypass probate.

6. **F** There is an oral will, but it is not as binding as a signed one and can lead to problems in some areas and states.

7. **F** It must be over a certain amount before you pay taxes on the money.

8. **F** They may refuse to follow the directives, but you would then get a new doctor.

9. **F** It can be oral, but it is not recommended.

10. **F** If you do not, the court system will choose one for your children.

11. **F** Every state has specific rules. A will or a durable power of attorney that is valid in one state could be void in another. Check with an attorney in your new state.

12. C

13. B

14. B

15. C

16. D

17. C

18. B

19. A

20. A

21. B

22. Medical Directive

23. Executor

24. Marital or Prenuptial

25. AB

26. Veterinary

27. Real Estate, IRAs, and 401(k) plans, which pass by beneficiary designation under the plan itself; life insurance, which again passes by beneficiary designation together with any payable on death accounts, which would pass directly to whoever is designated as a beneficiary; as well as joint accounts, which would pass by right of survivorship to the designated survivor.

28. Whole Body

29. Columbarium

30. TOD or Transfer on Death

31. Pallbearer

32. Incapacitated

33. No. Estate taxes are only imposed on individuals who have estates sufficiently large to trigger the tax.

34. No. The estate tax is tied up with the gift tax so that if you gift all your belongings before death, you might end up paying the same in the gift tax as you would simply leaving your property alone.

35. Yes, there are various ways, including:

    • Petitioning the court to make the desired change.

- Forming a new irrevocable trust with the desired change and having it purchase the assets from the existing irrevocable trust using an IOU that would be paid off at death, possibly from life insurance proceeds.

- When setting up an irrevocable trust, provide for a "protector" to be able to make a change. The protector cannot be the grantor, trustee, or beneficiary of the trust. It is someone who is named when the trust is formed and given the powers to make certain changes. Typically, you would name someone you trust, such as a family member (i.e., sister or brother) or a professional, such as your attorney or CPA. The protector cannot benefit themselves, but can only make changes as authorized by you, as grantor, when the trust is first established.

36. No. Once an individual reaches the age of majority (typically 18), the adult child should execute powers of attorney for financial and business affairs as well as their advanced legal directives. For example, an adult child heading off to college may want to execute the health care and financial documents so that if something happened to the child while at college, the parent would have the legal power to assist and make decisions.

37. No. The $12,000 annual gift tax exclusion is strictly a gift tax provision. Medicaid penalizes gifts of any size.

38. No. Not without a power of attorney, conservatorship, or letters testamentary.

39. Generally a grandparent. That knowledge alone could scare some people into getting their documents done.

Veterinary Schools
that Take Pets

Check online for other options as well. The fees that are mentioned below each program are for the care of your pet and for burial costs when your pet passes away.

Peace of Mind Program

School of Veterinary Medicine
Purdue University
800-213-2859
www.vet.purdue.edu/giving/giving/peaceofmind.html
Costs: This program requires a minimum $25,000 donation per pet.

Perpetual Pet Care Program

School Of Veterinary Medicine
Kansas State University
785-532-4013
http://www.vet.ksu.edu/depts/development/perpet/index.htm
Costs: This program requires a donation. Here is a breakdown of the costs:

Small companion animal: *$25,000*

Large companion animal: *$50,000*

Special needs animal: *$75,000*

Perpetual Care Program

College of Veterinary Medicine

University of Minnesota

612-624-1247

http://www.cvm.umn.edu/devalumni/perpetualcare/home.html

Costs: This program requires a minimum of a $25,000 gift.

Cohn Family Shelter for Small Animals

Oklahoma State University

College of Veterinary Medicine

405-744-6728

http://www.cvhs.okstate.edu/index.php?option=com_content&task=view&id=496&Itemid=605

Costs: The donation required for this program is as follows:

$10,000 for each bird

$15,000 for each cat

$25,000 for each dog

Stevenson Companion Animal Life-Care Center

College of Veterinary Medicine

Texas A&M University

979-845-1188

www.cvm.tamu.edu/petcare

Costs: This center has an enrollment fee of $1,000 for a small animal and $2,000 for a large animal. They have a scale of the minimum endowment required, which is calculated by the person's age. This information can be found on their Web site.

University of California Davis School of Veterinary Medicine Tender Loving Care for Pets Program (TLC)

UC Davis School of Veterinary Medicine Center for Animals in Society

530-752-7024

http://www.tlcforpets.org

Costs: $1,000 enrollment fee, plus a $30,000 endowment.

You can also locate animal rescue programs in your area that take pets. You can often find them on the Internet. You can contact the Estate Planning for Pets foundation, at **estateplanningforpets.org**, or you can send them a request for information, at 3150 E. Beardsley, Box 1091, Phoenix, AZ 85050. They can give you a directory of places to place your pet and suggestions on how to make those arrangements.

There are a number of animal sanctuaries nationwide that can help find a good home for your pet, should you die or become incapacitated. You can check out NB Pet Trusts, at **http://www.nbpettrusts.com/ sanctuaries.asp**, for a list of sanctuaries listed by state.

Bibliography

Bitticks, B., L. Benson, and D. Breininger,
The Senior Organizer Organizing for a Better Quality of Life,
Deerfield, Health Communications, 2006.

Cullen, M. and S. Irving,
Get It Together: Organize Your Records So Your Family Won't Have To,
Nolo, CA, 2007.

Hearn J. and N. Nielsen,
If Something Happens to Me, Provisio, Omaha, 2004.

Moody, E, Funerals,
http://www.ofmoody.com/miscellaneous/funeral.html,
retrieved October 7, 2008.

Pagano, R. For the Record:
A Personal Facts & Document Organizer, Five Star, Chandler, 2007.

Author Biography

John N Peragine, Ph.D., is a writer and classical musician. John holds a B.S. in psychology from Appalachian State University. His other books include, *eBay Income Advanced: How to Take Your eBay Business to the Next Level — For PowerSellers and Beyond* and *101 Recipes for Making Wild Wines at Home: A Step-by-Step Guide to Using Herbs, Fruits, and Flowers* (**www.atlantic-pub.com**). He loves to hike and spend time with his children. When John is not writing, he plays the piccolo with the Western Piedmont Symphony.

Index